CROSSWORD PUZZLES

their History and their Cult

Roger Millington
CROSSWORD PUZZLES
their History and their Cult

publishers since 1798

THOMAS NELSON INC., PUBLISHERS
Nashville   New York

Copyright © 1974 by Roger Millington

All rights reserved under International and Pan-American Conventions. Published by Thomas Nelson Inc., Publishers, Nashville, Tennessee. Manufactured in the United States of America.

First U.S. edition

Library of Congress Cataloging in Publication Data

Millington, Roger 1939–
  Crossword puzzles, their history and their cult.

  Bibliography: **p.**
  British ed. published in 1974 under title: The strange world of the crossword.
  SUMMARY: A history of the crossword with samples of some varieties of the puzzle.
  1. Crossword puzzles. [1. Crossword puzzles] I. Title.
GV1507.C7M488 1975   793.73'2   75–9505

Contents

	Foreword	7
ONE	The World's First Crossword	11
TWO	Mr. Simon and Mr. Schuster	14
THREE	The Craze	19
FOUR	The Ancestors of the Crossword	29
FIVE	The Big Money	46
SIX	A Lifetime of Puzzles	51
SEVEN	The World's Most Famous Crossword	57
EIGHT	The World's Toughest Puzzle Series	77
NINE	Crosswords With a Message	106
TEN	Variants of the Crossword	115
ELEVEN	Solving Them and Setting Them	128
TWELVE	Some Favourites	135
THIRTEEN	Some Records	156
	Bibliography	157
	Solutions	160

Foreword

This book started a couple of years ago when I was asked by an industrial company to compile a crossword containing an advertising message. My one and only attempt to create a crossword took two full days and was a hopeless failure. But it encouraged me to look at crosswords a little more closely and to try and discover who invented them and whether there are any easy rules for their construction.

The first thing I found was that so many people admit to solving crosswords on a fairly regular basis. So it was no surprise to come across a Gallup Survey claiming crosswords to be the most popular of all recreations. What was surprising was to find that this world-wide activity has been so overlooked by critics and researchers.

Why no psychological dissertations on the mental processes of clue solving?

Why no comparative literary studies between the clue constructions of *The Times* and *The Guardian*?

In due course, crosswords will no doubt come under the academic microscope. After all, over a hundred colleges in the United States now give courses in science fiction – and there aren't all that many science fiction works that can boast more ingenuity, more wit or more ideas than the daily crossword in *The Times*.

In the meantime this book attempts to piece together the history and progress of the crossword and to give a representative sample of some of the more unusual varieties of puzzle. Much of the material in it has not appeared in book form before and has necessitated much rummaging through dusty files—so at this point I submit my heartfelt thanks to the Staffs of the London Library, the British Museum Reading Room and the Hendon Newspaper Library.

The author is very grateful to the large number of people who have made this book possible. May I particularly mention:

The *St. Louis Post Dispatch* for permission to reproduce the world's first crossword, originally published in the New York *World*.

Simon & Schuster, Inc. for permission to reproduce the title page and opening puzzle from the first book of crossword puzzles.

Simon & Schuster, Inc. and the New York Times Studio for the photograph of Margaret Farrar.

The *Sunday Express* for permission to reproduce the first crossword published in Great Britain.

The Times for its photographs of the T-shirt crossword, and *The Times/Cutty Sark* crossword trophy; and for permission to reproduce puzzles in the Chapter, 'The World's Most Famous Crossword', and also for permission to reproduce Sir Max Beerbohm's crossword.

The Observer for permission to reproduce the puzzles by Torquemada, the puzzles of Ximenes and the puzzle 'In Memory of Ximenes'.

The Listener for permission to reproduce seven puzzles for the Chapter, 'The World's Toughest Puzzle Series', and for permission to include the Afrit puzzle in the final chapter.

Mr. R. G. Auckland, Editor of *The Falling Leaf,* for supplying the V-1 puzzle when I had given up all hope of ever locating a copy.

The Leicester Permanent Building Society and Frank Gayton Advertising Ltd. for the investment crossword.

Max Raynor of Combined Graphic Services Ltd. for permission to reproduce the C.G.S. puzzle.

The *Saturday Review* for permission to reproduce Double-Crostic Number 1.

David Bates for permission to include his Leadergram.

John Mathews for permission to include three Jax Squares.

The Associated Newspapers Group for permission to reproduce three puzzles by H. E. Dudeney and the Gilbert Frankau puzzle from the *Daily News*.

Penguin Books Ltd. for permission to reproduce six puzzles from the First and Second Penguin Problem Books.

Time & Tide for permission to reproduce 'The New 13 Across Movement' and 'Venture Into Space'.

Mr. Edmund Akenhead, Crossword Editor of *The Times*, for information on the first *Times* Crossword.

To literary agent Laurence Pollinger for personal reminiscences of Dick Simon and Max Schuster.

The New York Public Library and the Liverpool Record Office, Liverpool City Libraries, for information on Arthur Wynne.

The Curator of the Corinium Museum, Cirencester, for permission to reproduce the SATOR word square photograph.

The Editor of *Greece & Rome* for permission to include the illustration of the Stele of Moschion.

Gyles Brandreth for information on the National Scrabble Championship.

Methuen & Co. Ltd. for permission to reproduce an excerpt from 'Ximenes on the Art of the Crossword'.

The Appeal Secretary of the Royal College of Surgeons of England for permission to reproduce their advertisement in *The Times*.

David Tuhill for his surrealist visual joke on the crossword motif.

Clouds Studio of Soho and also Derek Mason for their painstaking work in re-drawing many puzzles.

Attempts have been made to trace all copyright holders.

1. The World's First Crossword

Arthur Wynne scratched his head searching for a new idea to include in his puzzle page for the magazine section of Sunday's New York *World*. For this 1913 Christmas edition he wanted something special. Up to now he had featured word squares, enigmas, hidden words, rebuses and anagrams. Playing around with a word square, it struck him that he could break with tradition—why should the across words necessarily be the same as the down words? Wynne sketched out a diamond shaped grid, reached for a dictionary, and a few hours later, the world's first crossword was born. It needed a name, so Wynne called it a 'Word-cross'.

This epoch-making puzzle appeared on December 21st 1913. The word 'Fun', which appears at the top of the puzzle, happened to be the title of the eight-page comic section in which the puzzle appeared. Its inventor probably didn't realise what he was starting. It was an instant success—no-one seemed to mind that two of the answers were identical—and he received enough letters from readers to persuade him to include a second puzzle the following Sunday. To his surprise, from the very first appearance of the puzzle he received crosswords compiled by his readers at the steady rate of six a week.

Not that the puzzle was popular with everyone. The *World*'s compositors hated it for the problems it created with their type make-ups. When it was dropped one Sunday, the paper was deluged with protests: 'The only thing I give a hang about on your page or in your Sunday magazine is the cross-word puzzle'. (Incidentally, it was quite some time before the hyphen dropped

11

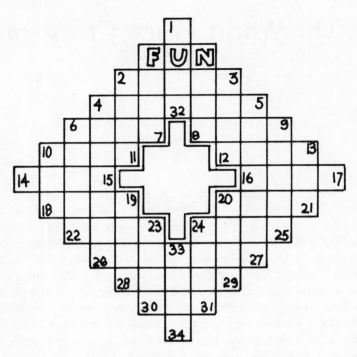

PUZZLE No. 1

The First Crossword Ever
(The solution may be found at the end of this book)

2–3. What bargain hunters enjoy.
4–5. A written acknowledgment.
6–7. Such and nothing more.
10–11. A bird.
14–15. Opposed to less.
18–19. What this puzzle is.
22–23. An animal of prey.
26–27. The close of a day.
28–29. To elude.
30–31. The plural of is.
8–9. To cultivate.
12–13. A bar of wood or iron.
16–17. What artists learn to do.
20–21. Fastened.
24–25. Found on the seashore.
10–18. The fibre of the gomuti palm.

6–22. What we all should be.
4–26. A day dream.
2–11. A talon.
19–28. A pigeon.
F–7. Part of your head.
23–30. A river in Russia.
1–32. To govern.
33–34. An aromatic plant.
N–8. A fist.
24–31. To agree with.
3–12. Part of a ship.
20–29. One.
5–27. Exchanging.
9–25. To sink in mud.
13–21. A boy.

out of the expression 'Cross-word'. For the rest of this book I will use the current hyphenless spelling, even when quoting from early accounts where the hyphen appears.)

So the crossword remained a regular feature in every Sunday's *World* – although to give it less space, the clues were set in agate, the smallest typeface available. As time went on, the crossword established its standard rectangular format and a list of formal rules – largely demanded by the *World*'s readers – was developed. Some puzzles had in effect consisted of several individual crosswords separated from each other within the main rectangle. Puzzlers insisted that all the clues must fully interlock. They refused, too, to countenance the use of foreign words in their weekly teaser. And they made life a little more difficult for puzzle compilers when they refused to accept silly abbreviations. One compiler, having problems making up a puzzle, had solved it by adopting GPJU as a four letter answer and giving as the clue: 'Grand Potentate of the Johnstown Union'.

Not much is known about the crossword's creator. He was born in Liverpool, the son of the Editor of the *Liverpool Mercury*. Arthur Wynne emigrated to America in about 1905 to enter newspaper work, and spent most of his working life with the Hearst newspaper chain. At one time he played the violin in the Pittsburgh Symphony Orchestra. He died in Clearwater, Florida, on January 14th 1945, leaving a widow, two daughters and a son.

For over ten years, the *World* remained the only newspaper to run crossword puzzles. One of the problems facing the newspaper was that typesetting errors kept creeping in. The difficulty was solved for a time by taking the proof sheet of the page as it came from the press and sending it up to the Editor's office for him to solve. In 1920 the *World* decided to hire a young Smith College graduate named Margaret Petherbridge. As we shall see, Miss Petherbridge was to be an important influence on the development of the crossword.

2. Mr. Simon and Mr. Schuster

On January 1st 1924, two ambitious young men arrived back at their tiny office celebrating their first morning in business together. To their dismay, the freshly painted sign on their door, 'Simon and Schuster, Publishers', bore an addition scrawled underneath – 'Of what?' No doubt the unknown humorist was aware that the publishing empire consisted of one typist and that the two publishers so far had no manuscripts to edit. By the end of the year the joke would be on him; for by then, Simon and Schuster would have three best-sellers, a score of employees and half a dozen offices.

Next evening Dick Simon dined at the home of a favourite Aunt, nicknamed Wixie. During the meal, Aunt Wixie asked her nephew for assistance. 'My daughter has become addicted to the crossword puzzles in the New York *World*. Where can I get a book of these puzzles to give her as a present?' Dick mentioned it next morning to Lincoln Schuster and after making a few enquiries they made the discovery that was to earn them a fortune. There was no such book. Dick gave Lincoln much the same look that Newton must have given the apple. 'A whole book of crosswords, eh? Well, we're supposed to be publishers.'

No slouches, they immediately sped across to the *World* to get in touch with Margaret Petherbridge and two of her co-editors, Prosper Buranelli and Gregory Hartswick. For an advance royalty of $25 each, the trio agreed to compile a book of puzzles. While they were in the newspaper office, the two publishers timidly called on 'F.P.A.', the *World*'s most famous columnist. F.P.A. had written several times of his enjoyment in solving crossword puzzles. Would he please write an introduction for the book? Franklin P. Adams certainly wouldn't. He contended that the book would be monotonous; it couldn't even pay the $75 royalty: and he didn't want his name associated with such a sure failure. When the crestfallen pair left his office, F.P.A. rushed down to Margaret Petherbridge. 'For heaven's sake, discourage them. They'll lose their shirts.' Margaret wasn't so lacking in confidence. She was already compiling the book.

Meanwhile, Simon and Schuster were checking on F.P.A.'s track record. They discovered that he was the man who advised the *New York Evening Mail* not to hire the great cartoonist Rube Goldberg at $50 a week. He had also warned Henry Sydnor Harrison to stick to rhyming and to quit writing his fabulously successful 'Queed'; and he had similarly implored Montague Glass to accept a mere $5,000 for all stage and dramatic rights to the equally successful 'Potash and Perlmutter'. Somewhat reassured, they decided to order a tiny edition of only 3,600 copies. But what printer in his right mind would extend credit to an unknown publishing company on a book of crossword puzzles? Luckily, they were able to find a printer who was himself a devoted fan of the *World*'s crosswords.

Simon and Schuster had already received the final manuscript when a well-wishing book distributor proffered his advice: 'If you must publish, at least do it under another name. Otherwise, you'll be a dead duck in the publishing business.' Grudgingly, they agreed that this was wise counsel and brought the book out under an alias – Plaza Publishing Company. The name Plaza was selected, as it happened to be the name of their telephone exchange. Unable to afford a publisher's representative, Dick Simon tramped from book dealer to dealer, soliciting orders. With only two exceptions, every bookseller was sceptical. One of the largest orders came from a major New York book store. The buyer, who was a personal acquaintance of Simon's, admitted later that he bought twenty-five copies out of friendship, although he hoped that he might just get rid of two or three. Later, that store alone sold thousands and thousands. By publication day, the advance sale was 800 copies plus a promise of 1,000 from a distributor.

PUZZLE No. 2

The opening puzzle in the first book of crosswords

HORIZONTAL

1. Pronoun.
3. Albumin from castor-oil bean
7. Exist.
9. Aged.
11. Negative.
12. Incite, hasten.
13. Remote.
15. Obstruction.
17. Bivalves.
21. Father.
23. Tree.
24. River in Italy.
25. Owners.
26. Printer's measure.
27. Tree.
28. Personal pronoun.
29. Legislative bodies.
31. Compact mass.
32. Moved rapidly.
34. Walk about.
35. Toss.
37. Small child.
39. Upon.
40. Small openings.
41. Act.

VERTICAL

1. Exclamation.
2. Fairy.
4. Preposition.
5. Plotter.
6. Pronoun.
7. Express generally.
8. Pronoun.
10. Obstruct.
12. Owns.
14. Disarranged.
15. Voluble talkativeness.
16. Above.
18. The bow of Vishnu.
19. Choose.
20. Assumed an attitude.
22. Limb.
24. Peer.
29. Sorrowful.
30. Rested.
31. Pale.
33. Incline the head.
34. Move.
35. Behold.
36. Exist.
38. Preposition.

16

THE CROSS WORD PUZZLE BOOK

An Anthology of Fifty Cross Word Puzzles
Selected as the Best of the Thousands That
Have Been Submitted to the New York World
Published Here Exclusively for the First Time
and Edited

By

PROSPER BURANELLI

F. GREGORY HARTSWICK

MARGARET PETHERBRIDGE

THE PLAZA PUBLISHING COMPANY
New York :: 1924

Title page of the first book of crossword puzzles

The first copy off the presses, suitably inscribed, went to Aunt Wixie and shortly before publication, Simon and Schuster blew the last of their money on a one-inch advertisement in the *World*:

Attention Crossword Puzzle Fans!
The First Book of Crossword Puzzles – $1.35
Your Money Back If Not 100% Satisfied!

$1.35 was quite a steep price for a book in those days – even though a freshly-sharpened pencil was attached to each copy. Schuster had persuaded the Venus Pencil Company into supplying these free as an advertising stunt. On the day of the book's appearance, April 10th 1924, F.P.A. gave it a welcome push by announcing in his column:

Hooray! Hooray! Hooray! Hooray!
The Crossword Puzzle Book is out today.

Within a day the publishers' telephone was jammed with orders . . . from fans who had seen the advertisement and from frantic booksellers who had done Simon and Schuster a favour by ordering a single copy and who were now anxious to order in bulk. Within three months, sales reached an astonishing 40,000 and edition after edition quickly appeared. The largest single order was for 55,000 copies. When a 25 c. edition followed, the same distributor made a single order for a quarter of a million copies, the biggest book order of its time. The distribution of free copies at a New York publishing convention started the fire of interest over the country. One Detroit dealer at the convention started a puzzle on the way home and on alighting from the train, sent a telegram for a hundred copies.

Quickly emerging from behind their cloak of anonymity, the publishers placed the company name of Simon and Schuster on a second volume of puzzles. For sentimental reasons, they kept the name of Plaza Publishing Company there as well; it stayed there on every title page until the Sixtieth Crossword Book when it was finally dropped for reasons now forgotten. By the time the company had reached its first birthday, three volumes of puzzles had appeared under the editorship of Miss Petherbridge with total sales of over 400,000 copies.

3. The Craze

Late in 1924 a man on a train travelling between New York and Boston counted the passengers who were engrossed in crossword puzzles. He found sixty percent of them hard at it. In the dining car, the steward and five waiters were struggling to find a five-letter word meaning 'serving to inspire fear'. A pity the waiters weren't working for the Baltimore and Ohio Railroad. With its fine record for public service, its Directors had already decided to put dictionaries on all its main line trains! Not to be outdone, the Pennsylvania Railroad printed crossword puzzles on the back of its dining car menus.

The biggest craze that America had ever seen was under way. Quick to sense the public pulse, newspapers jumped onto the bandwagon set in motion by Simon and Schuster. The New York *World* was first with a daily puzzle, composed by Gelett Burgess – best known for those immortal lines:

> I never saw a Purple Cow,
> I never hope to see one;
> But I can tell you, anyhow,
> I'd rather see than be one.

Burgess treated New Yorkers to another piece of doggerel when his first puzzle saw print on November 24th 1924:

> The fans they chew their pencils,
> The fans they beat their wives.
> They look up words for extinct birds—
> They lead such puzzling lives!

19

The last line was no exaggeration. The whole nation had puzzle mania. In the good old pre-crossword days, travellers used to lay in a supply of novels when boarding the steamer for Europe. Now they were sending to the dockside a suitcase full of puzzle books – one for each member of the party – dictionaries, an atlas, and that absolute essential, Roget's Thesaurus. Simon and Schuster were receiving daily telegrams directing that puzzle books complete with answers be sent without fail to departing steamers.

Engaged couples announced their good news by composing appropriate crosswords and sticking them in the local paper. The Rev. George McElveen, a Baptist pastor of Pittsburgh, was the first of many preachers to use the crossword puzzle to attract bigger congregations. He announced that a large blackboard would be placed in front of his pulpit. On it was an original puzzle and the audience were required to solve it before he would begin his sermon. The solved puzzle, needless to say, proved to be the text for his sermon. In Atlantic City, crosswords were distributed in church to stir interest in a current missionary campaign in China and Persia. Churchgoers were requested, however, not to solve the puzzles during the service.

In the New Year of 1925, Yale dropped Harvard with a staggering vowel to the jaw at an intercollegiate crossword tournament at the Hotel Roosevelt. The New York Police immediately issued a challenge to the Fire Brigade. Crowds filled Wanamaker's Auditorium to witness their heroes in a series of national tournaments.

Crosswords soon invaded the world of fashion. In January of 1925, a mill representative from New York gave a speech to report on the increased demand for checked patterns of all types and a silk company in Washington applied to register its crossword prints. A dress manufacturer did likewise for his natty crossword costume. At a fashion show in New York's 34th Street, a wholesaler displayed his new line of frocks embroidered with 4″ square puzzles. Every dress came with a book of puzzles – if the purchaser returned the book correctly solved, she was rewarded with a discount off future purchases. Over on 5th Avenue they were selling silver collar pins with a crossword motif at 50 c., together with solid gold crossword bracelets for $35.

In December, 1924, unaware that the craze was shortly to achieve similar magnitudes in Britain, *The Times* took pity on America. In an article headed AN ENSLAVED AMERICA, it noted that 'All America has succumbed to the crossword puzzle.' Guessing inaccurately, it continued: 'The crossword puzzle is by no means a new thing; in all likelihood it was known as long ago as the Civil War.' *The Times* felt that the crossword was 'a menace because it is making devastating inroads on the working hours of every rank of society.' How devastating? Well according to their New York correspondent, five million hours daily of American people's time – most of them nominally working hours – were being used in unprofitable trifling.

Perhaps *The Times* had failed to notice that the crossword was already here. Five weeks earlier, the *Sunday Express* had already used a puzzle submitted by Arthur Wynne of the New York *World*. This puzzle was offered to a London newspaper features syndicate as one of a batch of half a dozen. It required some alterations as the original puzzle employed an American spelling; however, it entitles Wynne to be regarded as the introducer of the crossword to both the United Kingdom and the United States.

Two months later, *The Times* reminded readers of its remarks on the American phenomena and added sadly: 'The account was hardly printed before the craze had crossed the Atlantic with the speed of a meteorological depression.' Evidently pleased with his metaphor, the leader writer continued: 'The nation still stands before the blast and no man can say it will stand erect again.' A comparison with jig-saw puzzles and detective stories followed, but 'the nearest analogue of the crossword puzzle is to be found in a maze such as Hampton Court affords. There, too, is the deliberate plunging into a mystery which we feel that we shall be clever enough to solve. There, too, are the false starts and the chastened return to the starting point; there, too, the tempting openings, the seductive corner leading time and again to blind alleys and mocking barriers; there, too, in the moment of despair, the appeal to the look-out man, perched aloft on his pedestal of superior wisdom, to give us a hint of the right way out'.

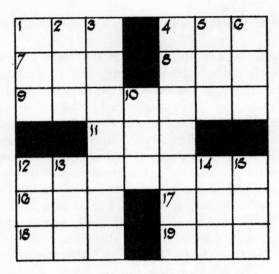

PUZZLE No. 3

The first crossword in Great Britain

HORIZONTALS

1. A coin (slang).
4. A tree.
7. Period.
8. Through.
9. Counters of votes.
11. Cosy little room.
12. Drainages.
16. Meaning three (prefix).
17. Snake-like fish.
18. An oriental coin.
19. Parched.

VERTICALS

1. Wager.
2. Mineral substance.
3. Eminent political figure.
4. Inflicted retribution.
5. A title.
6. Possesses.
10. Grassland.
12. Home of a certain animal.
13. Before (poetic form).
14. Always (poetic form).
15. Cunning.

Meanwhile, an increasing number of the Top People who read *The Times* were finding themselves relieved of their wallets by pickpockets who were able to evade suspicion by lounging in hotel lobbies pretending to complete crossword puzzles.

The crossword fad gained respectability on January 13th 1925, when *The New York Times* delightedly informed the world that Buckingham Palace had issued a statement testifying to Queen Mary's enthusiasm for the black and white squares. The Prime Minister turned out to be another fan: in the same month at a Press Club luncheon he talked of the bonds between politicians and the Press: 'There is another great bond. I as Prime Minister and you as journalists are engaged in the common work of trying to elevate the people of this country, and you are doing it today through that marvellous medium, the crossword puzzle. There is now hardly a man, woman or child in this country who is not familiar with the name of Eli. The fact that Asa was King of Judah can be concealed now from none. I should think that ninety percent of the people believed that there was but one Roman Emperor and that his name was Nero. They have learned that there is a mysterious bird in a far country of three letters and one snake of three letters.'

Less sure of the crossword's elevating role was the President of the Board of Trade who replied to a question by saying that he had no definite opinion as to their educational value. However, he might be able to say something a little later. Scholars at Princeton had few reservations. Professor Warner Fite, Professor of Logic, offered a prize to any student who could construct a puzzle with two completely different solutions. Over in the English Department, Professor Robert Root suggested establishing a course in the vocabulary of the English language employing a collection of crossword puzzles as a text book. Professor Fite claimed that the crossword offered a valuable exercise in logic. 'Whenever you have a given set of facts, you ask "Does it lead to one explanation or are various explanations possible?" If you have a set of synonyms that would give two complete and different puzzles, then you would have a case where you got two complete worlds out of one set of facts. That is more than a joke. It has considerable bearing on logic and on the

23

scientific explanation of the world. The question in any problem is always: is that always the only explanation?'

Some years after this suggestion of Fite's, 'Afrit' of *The Listener* managed to compose a puzzle in which every clue had two legitimate answers, thus making up two separate crosswords from a single set of clues. 'Ximenes' of *The Observer* repeated the feat and received many letters from readers asking for another. He found that it took him so long that he didn't do it a second time. In 1963 he did the trick in reverse when he presented the same diagram and most of the words of his first Ximenes crossword, this time employing a fresh set of clues. He hoped it might ring a bell among old solvers. It didn't. On another famous occasion, a Ximenes puzzle appeared one April 1st; he used the double solution joke for one quarter of the diagram. The alternative answers all interlocked with each other with the exception of one space; having got this far, you had to scrap your results and start off all over again to generate the correct set of answers. Considering that you weren't warned about this, it seems little short of miraculous that *The Observer* received forty correct solutions.

While considering the possibility of double-alternative solution, Professor Fite may well have considered the problem of the total possible number of ways of filling the squares of a crossword with any of twenty-six letters. This question came up recently in *The Times* during a comparison of the brain and the computer. A mathematician supplied the answer. Given a crossword with 120 white squares—the average size of a *Times* crossword—the number of solutions using any of twenty-six letters in any square is approximately equal to 24873 followed by two hundred and twenty-two noughts.

Professor Fite's liking for crosswords was echoed a few weeks after by James Lough, Dean of New York University, who saw the craze as a manifestation of mankind's old instinct for combat. 'Tired businessmen, college girls and office boys may think they are seeking to improve their minds when they find the correct solution to a puzzle. But they are doing that only as a by-product. What they really do is to work off a little of their primitive instinct for fighting—on the dictionary instead of batting their dearest enemy on the head or sticking a vicious elbow into the person who crowds them in the subway. While the fundamental instinct for combat still survives, it has become sublimated enough to enjoy a tussle with elusive synonyms.'

Other officials of the college agreed on the educational worth of the crossword but on the same day, the Carnegie Library in Pittsburgh announced that it had no crossword books on file and didn't intend to buy any. You can't blame them. The libraries had already discovered that the crossword puzzle was at odds with the advice given in the old *Librarian's Almanack*: 'Keep your books behind Stout Gratings, and in no wise let any Person come at them and take them from the Shelf except Yourself.' In England, the staff at Dulwich Library were being instructed to black out the crossword puzzles to prevent any person from keeping the newspaper for an unreasonable time. The Library Committee withdrew all dictionaries from the shelves to save them from wear and tear. The Liverpool Library Committee were less quick off the mark; a cunning Liverpudlian entering a prize contest sought to ensure his success by making things harder for his fellow competitors – he totally erased a significant and unusual word from a dictionary of considerable value. Faced with empty shelves in the libraries, competitors resorted to other means of seeking information; London Zoo announced in despair that it positively refused to answer any more telephone enquiries about the gnu, the emu or any other creature of three letters.

The Literature and Philology Department of Los Angeles Library took constructive steps to deal with the crossword mania. The latest dictionaries were kept at the reference desk, fastened to standing-height racks. These were available under supervision, but limited to a five minute use. They had to be relinquished if the librarians received telephone enquiries about unfamiliar words. The staff were forbidden to give opinions concerning correct answers, however. For a local newspaper contest on Bible verses, printed texts were provided in a pamphlet and direction was given to additional Bible texts when these were in demand. For a puzzle contest based on American Presidents a discarded loose-leaf encyclopedia was mounted and placed at the disposal of contestants in the History Room. Maps were mounted and made available for a similar geographical puzzle.

Librarians weren't the only people whose work was affected by the crossword. Mr. W. B. Barker, President of the British Optical Association, speaking at Staple Inn, drew attention to the varieties of headache arising from eye-strain and mentioned among others that variety caused by crosswords. A New York hospital had reported this trouble and qualified opticians in Britain were now meeting similar symptoms. The small type in which the clues were printed and the strain caused by the constant shifting to and fro of the eyes from the squares to the clues combined to overwork the sight whenever there was even a slight error of refraction. Qualified opticians could perform a valuable service, he advised, by warning the public against over-indulgence in the pastime.

The Headmaster of Rugby School was among those who saw the crossword as a threat to society. In a speech he contrasted the conversation of Englishmen and Frenchmen and expressed the view that the English were unsociable because they had never developed intelligence in conversation. The crossword puzzle was indicative of the English attitude to conversation. It was the laziest recreation and if men had not exhausted their brains without resorting to crosswords, they ought to be ashamed of themselves. 'This unsociable habit went through English society.'

The habit was unsociable enough to earn the disfavour of the law. In January, 1925, a New York Magistrate had to order court attendants, policemen and lawyers to cease pondering over crosswords when he convened the traffic court one Monday morning. The Magistrate had mounted the bench to discover twenty-one people circled around a table before him. 'Are all these people complainants?' he asked an attendant who said something about 'four letters meaning elevated' before glancing up and gasping in the next breath, 'Attention! The Court!'

'What are they doing?' queried the beak.

'Solving crossword puzzles.'

'Tell them to stop at once.'

Defendant, John Smietanka then informed the Magistrate that crossword puzzles were responsible for his failure to return to court several days ago and pay a fine imposed a week earlier. He was sentenced to the workhouse for ten days.

A few evenings later, three men were enjoying supper separately in a New York restaurant. One of them had a Simon and Schuster puzzle book propped against the sugar bowl. Drawn as by a magnet, the other two joined him. Midnight came but the three men were engrossed. At two in the morning, with all the other patrons long departed, the waiters were piling the chairs on the tables and sweeping the floor. The three puzzlers refused to budge. An hour later, the demented restaurant proprietor called the police and the ringleader was arrested. Next morning the judge gave him ten days in a four-letter word meaning 'place of detention'. The crossword fan was delighted. 'That's great! Now I'll have a chance to work puzzles in peace and quiet.'

Judge Sabath in Chicago faced an irate housewife in Mrs. Mary Zaba, when she charged that her husband was so busy solving crossword puzzles that he didn't have time to support her. Mr. Zaba agreed that he had fallen victim to the lure of the clues but denied that they had made him forget his marital responsibilities. Judge Sabath's ruling appears to have been a wise compromise: Zaba was instructed to ration himself to three puzzles a day and to devote the rest of the time to his domestic duties.

Mrs. Koerner of Brooklyn was less lucky. Her husband, a twenty-seven year old adjuster for the New York Telephone Company, asked her one evening for help with his crossword.

'I'm tired, and I'm going to lie down for a while,' she replied.

A few minutes later, the bedroom door opened and she was faced by her husband brandishing a pistol. As she screamed, she was aware of a blinding flash, a loud explosion and a burning sensation on her temple. She fled from the house, to be followed by her husband who fired a second time as she ran. Safely around the corner, she heard a third shot. Returning a few minutes afterwards with two detectives, she found her husband dead with a bullet through his heart.

The craze took a bizarre turn in Budapest in 1926 when Julius Antal, a waiter in one of the biggest coffee houses committed suicide. In his pocket a crossword was found with the following

Cross-Word Puzzles Appeal to 30 Million Adults, Poll Sho~

Rated Number One 'Indoor' Game; Checkers, Bingo, Poker Next; 15 Million Adults Play Bridge

By GEORGE GALLUP
Director, American Institute of Public Opinion

PRINCETON, N. J., Feb. 24—In the course of
U.S. adults will have tried their h
word puzzle than will hav
leisure time activity

This interesting f
from a nationwide
ducted by the Gal
mine the istep
in sports

Hig
mill
to

America's Number One Pastime
A Gallup Report headline – February, 1959.

laconic note:

'The solution will give you the exact reasons for my suicide and also the names of the persons interested.'

Police code experts were unable to solve the cipher and were obliged to call for the local crossword champions.

But if solving crosswords was difficult for the police it was no easier for the General Post Office. Early in 1925, a reader of *The Times* wrote bitterly to the Editor: 'I had always been brought up to believe that the Post Office took pleasure in delivering all possible packets entrusted to it, and particularly prided itself on the ingenuity with which it could decipher difficult addresses. There was a tale that a letter bearing the simple inscription 'March 25th' was safely delivered to the house of a well-known Lady Day, and other similar stories are told. Apparently, however, the Post Office has lost its taste for conundrums. Recently, I posted an envelope with the address embodied in a small crossword puzzle. It was a very easy puzzle with the 'lights' designed to assist rather than to baffle the solver, and the important squares indicated in coloured ink. It has been returned to me, marked firmly *No address!*'

28

4.
The Ancestors of the Crossword

The crossword has two forerunners: the acrostic and the word square. The one that has enjoyed the most continuous popularity is the acrostic. Originally, in an acrostic verse the first letters of each line spelt a word or phrase when read downward. Later, acrostics were developed in which the central or final letters made up a message. The word itself, which is of Greek origin meaning 'first letter verse' was first applied to the verses of the Erythraean sibyl, or prophetess, whose verses were written on leaves. In the best crossword traditions, these prophecies were notoriously obscure but were so devised that when the leaves were sorted, their initial letters always made up an appropriate word.

In his treatise, 'De Divinatione', Cicero remarks that, 'The verses of the sybils are distinguished by that arrangement which the Greeks call Acrostic; where from the first letters of each verse in order, words are formed which express some particular meaning; as in the case with some of Ennius's verses, the initial letters of which make "which Ennius wrote".'

Twelve poems of the Old Testament are written in acrostic form, the device being popular with Hebrew poets whose compositions consist of twenty-two stanzas beginning with successive letters of the Hebrew alphabet. The 119th Psalm is the best example. Here the translators who prepared the Authorised Version succeeded in heading each stanza with the appropriate letter: Aleph, Beth, Gimel, Daleth, and so on.

The figure of a fish preserved on many monuments in the Roman Catacombs is a reminder of the secret acrostic invented by the early Christian martyrs. The Greek word for fish is ιχθυς,

29

and served to mean Jesus Christ, the Son of God, the Saviour:

$$
\begin{array}{ll}
Ιησους— & \text{Jesus} \\
Χριστος— & \text{Christ,} \\
θεου— & \text{of God,} \\
Ϋιος— & \text{Son,} \\
Σωτηρ— & \text{Saviour.}
\end{array}
$$

Latin poets also wrote acrostic verse while the ninth century English poet, Cynewulf, has several acrostic runes to his name. In the Middle Ages, abecedarian hymns were designed as an aid to memorising the alphabet. When Good Queen Bess was on the throne, Sir John Davies, the poet and statesman, published twenty-six 'Hymnes of Astraea' in which the initial letters spelled out ELISABETHA REGINA in each hymn.

By the time of Addison, single, double and triple acrostics were in vogue – he writes about them in the sixtieth number of *The Spectator*. In the double acrostic, the final letters as well as the initials spell a word. In a triple acrostic, the central letters create a third word. Sometimes the acrostic is meant to be read downward, sometimes upward. A particularly clever variety is the Telestich in which the initial letters spell one word while the final letters compose a word of the opposite meaning:

> Unite and untie are the same – so say yoU
> Not in wedlock, I ween, has this unity beeN.
> In the drama of marriage each wandering gouT
> To a new face would fly – all except you and I –
> Each seeking to alter the spell in their scenE.

Perhaps the most delightful story of acrostic versifying is that concerning a sailor called Oliver who, after the War of American Independence, visited his cousin, the American officer and traitor, Benedict Arnold. As a reward for surrendering West Point, Arnold was now a Brigadier General serving the King. Oliver was well known for his ability to create off-the-cuff compositions and was requested by Arnold to make up a poem to amuse a group of English officers. He immediately greeted his unlovely cousin with this excellent curse:

30

Born for a curse to virtue and mankind,
*E*arth's broadest realm ne'er knew so black a mind.
*N*ight's sable veil your crimes can never hide,
*E*ach one so great, 'twould glut historic tide.
*D*efunct, your cursed memory will live
*I*n all the glare that infamy can give.
*C*urses of ages will attend your name,
*T*raitors alone will glory in your shame.

*A*lmighty vengeance sternly waits to roll
*R*ivers of sulphur on your treacherous soul:
*N*ature looks shuddering back with conscious dread
*O*n such a tarnished blot as she has made.
*L*et hell receive you, riveted in chains,
*D*oomed to the hottest focus of its flames.

The Victorians with their great appetite for word games were the first to employ acrostics as puzzle exercises, the first in print being described as an 'Acrostic Charade' when it appeared in *The Illustrated London News* of August 30th 1856. This double acrostic puzzle was devised by the Rev. J. Bradley who hid under the pseudonym of 'Cuthbert Bede'.

PUZZLE No. 4

The first printed acrostic puzzle

THE WORDS

A mighty centre of woe and wealth;
   A world in little, a kingdom small.
A tainted scenter, a foe to health;
   A quiet way for a wooden wall.
Find out these words as soon as you can, sir,
And then you'll have found the Acrostic's answer.

THE LETTERS

Untax'd I brighten the poor man's home—
   My wings wave over the beauty's brow—
I steal by St. Petersburgh's gilded dome—
   While Bomba's subjects below me bow.
A Cook has reason to dread my name,
Though I carry the tidings of pride and shame.

31

Bradley's solution is especially noteworthy as he provides a third verse as an explanation of his clues (see solutions at the end of this book). Incidentally, he makes no claim to have invented the double acrostic, but simply refers to it as having been 'lately introduced'.

In the early 1920's, H. E. Dudeney, the great English compiler of puzzles, made a literary discovery that suggests that one of the first inventors of the double acrostic was Queen Victoria! In 1861 a book was published entitled 'Victorian Enigmas; or, Windsor Fireside Researches: being a Series of Acrostics Enigmatically Propounded'. In this book the author, Charlotte Eliza Capel, includes a double acrostic which she claims to have been written by the Queen for the Royal children. The puzzle was formulated, according to Charlotte, in 1856 – the year when the Rev. Bradley says they were 'lately introduced'. If Queen Victoria really did invent this ancestor of the crossword, no doubt she would have been intrigued to learn that in later years her great-great-grand-daughter, Princess Margaret, was to win a book prize as a result of entering a *Country Life* crossword competition.

PUZZLE No. 5

Queen Victoria's double acrostic puzzle

A city in Italy.
A river in Germany.
A town in the United States.
A town in North America.
A town in Holland.
The Turkish name for Constantinople.
A town in Bothnia.
A city in Greece.
A circle on the globe.

The initials form the name of a town in England and the final (read upwards) what that town is famous for.

The literary curiosity that combined with the acrostic to inspire the crossword puzzle was the word square. The most famous of all is the splendid SATOR word square which has the unusual distinction that it is the only one that can be read as an intelligible sentence.

```
ROTAS
OPERA
TENET
AREPO
SATOR
```

It can be translated as 'The sower Arepo holds the wheels at work', or 'Arepo the sower holds the wheels with force'. 'Arepo' is the only non-Latin word; in Celtic it means 'a plough'. The square holds an additional superiority over later word squares in that it can be read four ways: from left to right, top to bottom, and bottom to top. Its origin has long mystified scholars and was the cause of a lively and enjoyable correspondence in *The Times*. In January, 1925, a reader wrote asking if anyone could explain the history of the square. Two days later, the Rev. W. Hopkinson pointed out that in the church of Great Gidding in the diocese of Ely is an octagonal piece of oak bearing the device:

```
        1614
        SATOR
  E     AREPO     R
        TENET
        OPERA
        ROTAS
```

When he was vicar of that parish in 1868 at the time of the church's restoration, Hopkinson wrote to *Notes & Queries* and received the suggestion that E.R. might be the initials of the incumbent in 1614. So it turned out: Edward Rumbolt. Hopkinson felt that the inscription alluded to his manner of conducting the service:

SAT ORARE POTEN? ET OPERA ROTAS

'Are you able to pray sufficiently? And you gabble through the church services'. In explanation, Hopkinson added that the word 'opera' was used in medieval Latin with respect to church services. A fortnight later, however, the Rev. T. D. Hicks of Aston Rowant, Oxfordshire, pointed out that starting from the S's, one finds in four ways:

SATOR OPERA TENET

'The creator maintains his works.' This is also an anagram of:

PATER NOSTER A ET O (Alpha et Omega)

Hicks suggested that this was the source of strong magic attributed to the charm in the Middle Ages, cleverly hidden under a covering sentence of good plain Latin with the scriptural ring to it. Four years passed before the square entered the correspondence columns again. After it had popped up in the *Manchester Guardian*, Hicks in April 1929 wrote again to *The Times* to restate his theory. This was rapidly followed by an anonymous reader who felt it was a cryptogram for 'Pray without ceasing, Our Father, the beginning and the end'. But four days later a different offering came from Sir Ernest Wallis Budge who referred to a work entitled 'Incantamenta Magica' by Heim and claimed that the words were a contraction for:

SAT ORARE POTEN(TER) ET OPERA(RE) R(ATI)O T(U)A S(IT)

He regarded these words as the remains of a Latin hymn which the early Roman Christians used in their religious exercises. The SATOR word square could be found in Coptic magical texts of the sixth century and was introduced into Abysinnia by the Portuguese of the fourteenth century. Moreover, in the Ethiopian Book of the Dead, 'Lefa fa Sedek', it is said to represent the five nails of the cross, forming the mighty spell that enabled a man to escape condemnation on Judgement day. Finally, the writer added, the recital of the charm in Glamorgan is supposed to cure the bite of a mad dog.

Next day a letter signed Bloston of Aldgate made an alternative proposition: 'May there not be another explanation of this anagram? Let anyone try with Latin words of the same length to make an anagram on the same model which shall yield grammatical sense, and he will find it exceedingly difficult, for reasons which will soon dawn on him as he proceeds with the attempt. Many letters of the alphabet will have to be ruled out at once, and not many will be left to play with at the end. SATOR and

34

ROTAS, two common words, must have been known as palindromes immemorially. TENET is one of the few palindromes possible in the middle; OPERA follows naturally, and to fill up, one must fall back on the unintelligible AREPO. Let unbelievers, before rejecting this theory, produce another anagram on the same model; they will find it very hard.'

Sure enough, no-one rose to meet the challenge but the Rev. Hicks made another appearance, this time to throw the gauntlet to Sir Ernest Wallis Budge by asking if POTEN, OPERA, RO, TA and S were used anywhere else as contradictions for POTENTER OPERARE, RATIO, TUA and SIT. Sir Ernest ducked that one when he replied that the square is of wholly pagan origin and that the Christians adopted it. Reminding us that the literature on the subject is very extensive, he could not find any writer save Heim and the Rev. Hicks who were prepared to give it a Christian character.

After printing a few other letters on the topic, the Editor of *The Times*, perhaps weary of the whole business, summarised the correspondence on the leader page and ventured the hope that the exchanges had now finished. Some hope! Hicks was back next day.

'Sir, in his letter of April 13, Sir Ernest Wallis Budge told us that he regards the palindrome as the remains of an early Latin hymn, and that Heim is most probably correct. I am still more puzzled when Sir Ernest says in his later letter "the palindrome is wholly of pagan origin". Sir Ernest Wallis Budge knows so much more than I do that I feel rather like a fourth-form boy trying to argue with the headmaster.'

The crossfire continued when Sir Ernest penned another letter advancing further reasons why the formula is a magic spell of non-Christian origin. Two more days and we find Hicks making another sally, but by now the arguments weren't really getting anywhere and one wonders if anyone was reading the letters other than the two opponents and the Editor.

But evidently someone was. Writing from the Old Palace, Oxford, R. A. Knox silenced the contest when he wondered if the square was an anagram for a spell to ward off evil spirits:

35

RETRO SATANA TOTO OPERE ASPER

'Begone, Satan, cruel in all thy works.' Alternatively, Knox thought it might be a prayer addressed to some particular saint:

O PATER ORES PRO AETATE NOSTRA

'O Father, pray for our times.' Or, asked Knox, shall we regard it as a piece of work addressed to the clergy?

ORA OPERARE OSTENTA TE PASTOR

'Pray, work, show thyself a pastor.' If that one wasn't felt by its clerical target, both the Rev. Hicks and Sir Ernest must have winced at Knox's final shot: There is no difficulty in finding a multitude of anagrams. The trouble is to prove that any one was put there on purpose. In fact, if I may express my meaning anagrammatically,

O ROT! PREPARE TO STATE A REASON

At the time of this inconclusive correspondence, the earliest known version of the SATOR word square was an inscription on a piece of painted wall plaster discovered in 1868 on the site of the Roman city of Corinium, now Cirencester. This is believed to date from the second, third or fourth century A.D.. In the 1920's a German scholar noted that the letters could be arranged:

```
          A
          P
          A
          T
          E
          R
APATERNOSTERO
          O
          S
          T
          E
          R
          O
```

The A's and O's stand for *alpha* and *omega*, the beginning and

36

The SATOR word square found at Cirencester

the end. This re-arrangement of the letters lead to the assumption that the square was Christian in origin and that it was used as a secret sign by which the early Christians could recognise each other in times of persecution. When further examples were found by archeologists in 1933 at Doura-Europa, most scholars were in agreement that the device was a Christian invention.

However, the whole academic applecart was upset in 1936 when the square was found inscribed on the plaster of a column at Pompeii, dating it to 79 A.D. at the latest – the date of the city's destruction by Vesuvius. Five problems immediately presented themselves. It seems improbable that there would be Christians at Pompeii at so early a date. Even if there were, why were they writing in Latin when Greek was the accepted language then used in Christian worship? How could they use the symbolism of *alpha* and *omega* prior to the writing of the Apocalypse? Further, the cross does not appear as a widely used Christian symbol until the third century. And finally, the disguising of Christian symbols within cryptograms does not generally appear until the third century. It seems fitting that the world of crossword puzzledom begins with a puzzle that has so far defied solution. Readers wishing to be in possession of more of the clues are recommended to get hold of *The Journal of Ecclesiastical History*, Vol. 2, January-April 1951, and read 'The Origin and Date of the Sator Word Square', a fascinating account by Professor Donald Atkinson.

*   *   *

Less ingenious than the Sator word square, but no less potent as a magic charm, is the cabalistic device ABRACADABRA, generally written in a triangular array on parchment and suspended from the neck by a linen thread as an antidote against agues. Possibly, it was constructed from the opening letters of the Hebrew words Ab (Father), Ben (Son), and Ruach Acadash (Holy Spirit). Part of its power is ascribed to the fact that the word ABRACADABRA can be read in so many ways when set in an array.

How many ways can you read the word ABRACADABRA in this triangular array?

```
A B R A C A D A B R A
A B R A C A D A B R
A B R A C A D A B
A B R A C A D A
A B R A C A D
A B R A C A
A B R A C
A B R A
A B R
A B
A
```

Before leaving the ancient world, it is interesting to note that elaborate word squares were widespread in the civilisation of Greece. The example shown here dates from about 300 A.D. Known as the 'Stele of Moschion', it was found in Egypt and is believed to have been erected by Moschion, an Egyptian familiar with the Greek tongue.

Incised on the surface of an alabaster monument, it features 1,521 squares (39 × 39), each holding one Greek letter. The trick in reading the puzzle is to start at the centre, proceed right, left, up or down, as far as the margin – and then turn at right angles and continue to the corner. The message then reads: 'Moschion to Osiris, for the treatment which cured his foot'.

You read the same text, in fact, if you start at the centre and take any zigzag course proceeding by alternate right and left turns. Other poems on the monument reveal Moschion's great satisfaction with his skill in creating the puzzle. A little thought will show that he scarcely deserves such self-congratulation: a similar square is easily developed from any text as long as you start off with an uneven number of letters.

More interesting to the archeologist are the many hundreds of word squares designed in what is known as the 'stoichedon' style. These were first invented in Athens in the sixth century B.C. Stoichedon inscriptions read only horizontally, the rectangular

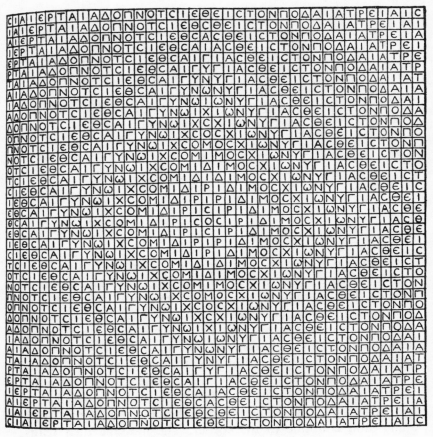

The Stele of Moschion

arrangement being purely for artistic effect. If the sculptor found a line finishing in the middle of a word, that was regarded as just hard luck on the reader – the visual appearance of the inscription was held as being more important than mere readability. This typographic conceit, nevertheless, proves invaluable to the historian who wishes to restore the text of a damaged stone tablet. As R. P. Austin explains in an article on stoichedon inscriptions in the May 1939 issue of *Greece & Rome*, 'the engraver, by arranging the letters in this rigorous manner so that each line had exactly the same number, enables us to see at a glance how many letters have to be supplied to make good the part which is lost.

The result is that the restoration of the missing letters can be achieved with ease and certainty. The scholar who has an expert knowledge of Greek inscriptions will find the filling of these gaps as easy as solving the simplest crossword. He gets his clues from the remainder of the lines, and, since he knows how many letters are lost, he has an almost perfect control of his solution'.

One ancient puzzle that has so far defied analysis is the 'Phaestus Disc' which was found on the island of Crete and which now resides at the Archeological Museum of Johns Hopkins University in Baltimore, Maryland. Believed to date from about 200 B.C., this terra cotta disc contains pictured writing arranged in a spiral array. As the writing has never been deciphered, it is anyone's guess as to whether the text starts at the rim and works inwards or whether it starts at the centre and runs outwards. It is thought that it may be a religious hymn and that the disc was imported into Crete from Lycia in Asia Minor. It is also likely that the disc represents a die intended for the mass production of similar word arrays.

Like the acrostic, the word square achieved considerable popularity in Victorian newspapers and magazines. It wasn't long before magazine editors discovered that the device could be turned into a puzzle by supplying readers with simple clues leading to the construction of a square. Numerous examples of such puzzles can be found in *St. Nicholas*, the American journal for children, founded in 1873. In its puzzle pages, this much-loved paper featured other geometrical forms based on the idea of the word square. Word diamonds were the most popular, although there were occasional stars, twin diamonds and stair-case designs – many of them submitted by precocious readers of eleven or twelve years of age.

Squares composed of three-, four-, or five-letter words are, of course, relatively easy to produce. The problem is to create arrays using longer words. Dudeney complained in 1925 that very few seven-letter word squares had been constructed and that he had never seen a good one of eight letters. But in his Appendix to the Dover Publications edition of C. C. Bombaugh's *Oddities & Curiosities of Words & Literature*, Martin Gardner provides several successful examples:

41

```
N E S T L E S        P R E P A R E
E N T R A N T        R E M O D E L
S T R A N G E        E M U L A T E
T R A I T O R        P O L E M I C
L A N T E R N        A D A M A N T
E N G O R G E        R E T I N U E
S T E R N E R        E L E C T E D

M E R G E R S        S H E A V E D
E T E R N A L        H O S T I L E
R E G A T T A        E S T A T E S
G R A V I T Y        A T A X I C S
E N T I T L E        V I T I A T E
R A T T L E R        E L E C T O R
S L A Y E R S        D E S S E R T
```

These were supplied to Martin Gardner by Dmitri Borgmann,
an American word puzzle expert. Gardner reproduces an 8 × 8
square and also the following remarkable 9 × 9 array:

```
F R A T E R I E S
R E G I M E N A L
A G I T A T I V E
T I T A N I T E S
E M A N A T I S T
R E T I T R A T E
I N I T I A T O R
E A V E S T O N E
S L E S T E R E D
```

Seven of the words here are in Webster's unabridged dictionary.
Retitrate means to titrate again. Eavestone is a locality in Yorkshire. This particular square was compiled by Wayne Goodwin
of Chicago in 1928, although it is far from being unique –
Borgmann claims that about nine hundred 9 × 9 squares have
been constructed in English! Immortality awaits the constructor
of the first 10 × 10 square.

The first word square puzzles with clues in verse appear to have
been compiled by H. E. Dudeney. This example dates from
about 1890:

'The Abbey' – A word square by H. E. Dudeney
'Twas spring. The abbey woods were decked with
  second.
The abbot, with his *fifth*, no trouble reckoned;
But shared the meats and *seventh* which every man
Who loves to feast has *first* since time began.
Then comes a stealthy *sixth* across the wall,
Who *fourths* the plate and jewels, cash and all,
And ere the abbot and the monks have dined,
He *thirds*, and leaves no trace or clue behind.

   Dudeney's American rival, the master puzzlist Sam Loyd
(1841–1911), produced only a handful of teasers based on word
arrays. The following two puzzles appear in the 'Mammoth
Cyclopedia of Puzzles', edited by Loyd's son in 1914.
   'The Little Brown Jug' was an early Sam Loyd puzzle, created
for the benefit of a temperance organisation. The problem is to
determine just how many ways one can read the warning 'Red
Rum & Murder'. Commence at any of the R's, including those
inside the diamond, and spell the phrase by moving up or down,
left or right, or diagonally to an adjacent letter.

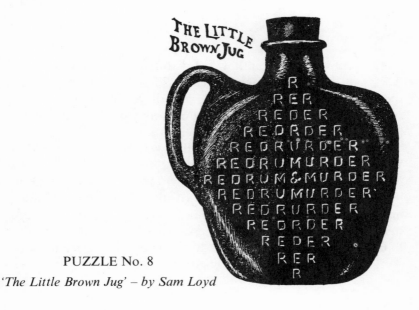

PUZZLE No. 8

'The Little Brown Jug' – by Sam Loyd

PUZZLE No. 9

'Alice in Wonderland' – another Sam Loyd creation

The problem is this: in how many different ways can you read Alice's question, 'Was it a cat I saw?' Start at any of the W's, spell by moving to adjacent letters until you reach the C, then spell back out to the border again. You may move up and down, left and right.

Was it from the acrostic and the word square that Arthur Wynne got his inspiration for the first crossword puzzle in the New York *World*? It seems almost certain. Wynne told his journalistic colleagues that he got the idea from children's magazines he had read as a child in Liverpool. The probability is that *St. Nicholas* was among these magazines; it was published in Britain as well as in America. In this paper the horizontal clues to word-squares were, in fact, usually described as 'cross-words'.

It is tempting to think that the puzzle below is one that young Arthur sweated over as a boy. It appeared in the issue of December 1880, and is the earliest that I have come across using the now familiar Down and Across clues – although earlier examples may possibly be discovered by anyone with facilities for searching through each previous copy of the magazine.

PUZZLE No. 10

The puzzle that inspired the crossword?

DOUBLE DIAMOND

Across

1. In Chinaman.
2. A pert townsman.
3. An old word meaning the crown of the head.
4. The Indian name for a lake.
5. A prize given at Harvard University.
6. A masculine nickname.
7. In Chinaman.

Downward

1. In Chinaman.
2. A capsule of a plant.
3. A printer's mark showing that is interlined.
4. Men enrolled for military discipline.
5. A fibrous product of Brazil.
6. The first half of a word meaning very warm.
7. In Chinaman.

5. The Big Money

The crossword craze was only a few days old when one New York newspaper realised its potential as a vehicle for competitions. The '*Evening Graphic*' ran the first crossword prize contest in December 1924. Next month they ran a contest in twenty-six instalments – one puzzle a day. Entry was free and there were 2,619 cash prizes ranging from five to five thousand dollars.

At the time, the novelist Carolyn Wells was puzzle editor for another New York paper, *The Midweek Pictorial* – a picture magazine. Not to be outdone, she gave prizes for the best crosswords constructed by readers, based on pictures in the current issue of the paper.

Prize competitions were quickly adopted in Britain. By the end of 1926, one Sunday newspaper was seeking to attract new readers by advertising that it was possible to win £8,000 every week by entering the crossword contests in its pages. Some of the contests were sponsored by the papers themselves; most of them were, in effect, lotteries set up by private companies. As a money-making venture for the sponsors, few ideas have ever paid such dividends. Lottery puzzles could be recognised by the unusually large number of black squares – in a conventional crossword the black boxes rarely exceed a sixth of the total number of squares in the diagram. The clues are cleverly worded in a lottery puzzle to give the possibility of alternative answers. For instance, the clue 'You look forward to getting this when you are in hospital' can be equally answered by BETTER or LETTER. If the first letter of the answer is unchecked that is, surrounded by black squares, then achieving the correct result is a matter of pure chance. With a large number of such clues in one puzzle, the number of possible entries becomes immense; even if each entry costs the competitor merely a few pennies, the sponsor stands to collect far more than the prize money paid for the handful of 'correct' results. It's no good arguing with the judges that your answers fit the clues better than the ones that were chosen as correct; it is always a condition of entry that there shall be no dispute.

Just how much money could be made by this particular racket was indicated by an account published in *The Spectator* in November, 1926. Three men formed a syndicate; each contributed a capital of £1,000. They then compiled a lottery puzzle, placed it in the advertisement space of several Sunday papers and hired a group of girls to handle the entry forms and postal orders. On the first Monday they received five entries. Not an encouraging response as one paper alone had charged £250 to publish the puzzle. A return of five shillings on their investment was far from cheerful. On Thursday a whole vanload arrived and the happy businessmen required suitcases to carry the postal orders to the bank. Within three months they were spending £2,000 a week on advertising space, had a staff of 35 girls and were each drawing £100 a week profit.

And they were just one of many syndicates in the business. It was a regular sight to see the entire back page of a Sunday paper taken up with contest puzzles.

One newspaper in New York coined the expression **PRUZZLES** to describe this type of crossword (**PR**ize p**UZZLE**).

This PRUZZLE Deal Gotcha Guessing?
Thought it was easy didn't you? Well, despite the fact that thousands of Brooklyn Eagle readers sent in their solutions to the first Eagle **PRUZZLE**, nobody got the correct answer!

The main roadblock seemed to be 23 Across. Almost every entry had 'Pain' when they should have used

'Vain'. The clue for 23 Across was: 'To have to wait in
_____ in the dentist's office is infuriating'. The correct
answer: 'Vain'.

Not all the money from these contests went into the wrong
pockets. The Treasurer of the Greater London Fund for the
Blind ran crossword contests in the newspapers to raise funds.
The entrance fee each week was a shilling – and the prize was
£1,000. The takings amounted to over £1,000 a day. During the
holidays, the promoter issued a notice explaining that the contest would be discontinued for a few weeks but would readers
still send their weekly donation. The response? Three shillings
and sixpence!

In the United States, the postal authorities took a dim view of
what they correctly regarded as a lottery. In Britain the law was
not too sure. Not until 1931 were summonses brought against
Allied Newspapers Limited to challenge the legality of crossword
puzzles in the *Sunday Chronicle*. Much to the relief of the press,
the case was dismissed in Manchester Police Court.

Later in the 30's, another Sunday paper was prosecuted for
running a lottery and won its case. The decision was reversed
when the police appealed against the ruling. Lively scenes ensued
in the High Court when learned counsel argued the merits of
various answers to ambiguous clues of the type described above.

A 17-year-old boy's prize money was handed over to the
administration of Westminster County Court in April 1935 when
the question arose as to how it should be dealt with under the
Trustee Act. The Judge granted an application by a solicitor to
give the boy £20 for his immediate needs; £100 to apprentice him
to a firm of motor engineers for two years, the firm to be paid £1
a week; and £1 a week to be paid to his father for the boy's
maintenance.

Dictionary publishers made a fortune during the era of the
great prize contests. £500 WON! £1000 SHARED! boasted the
headline of a display advertisement for the *Waverley Modern
Dictionary*. Mrs. M. Carwithen of Southampton testified: 'I
won £500 outright in the *Sunday Chronicle* Crossword Competition . . . I never use any other dictionary than the Waverley',

while Mr. B. J. Owlett of Kendal added: 'By the aid of your valuable Dictionary I have shared in the £1,000 Crossword Prize of *The People*. As the publisher helpfully pointed out, 'you can never be quite sure of your solutions if you have only an ordinary dictionary to help you'.

Having bought your dictionary and discovered all the alternative answers to each clue, it became painfully clear that the more different entries you sent in, the greater your chances of winning. Did this mean you had to buy umpteen copies of the paper in order to cut out the coupons? Of course not! You just sent your money to Hosking Edwards, The Coupon King of Huddersfield. He could supply blank coupons from any penny paper at the rate of 8/– a hundred, thereby saving you one shilling and fourpence, less the cost of your stamp.

To save yourself the labour of looking up answers in the dictionary, it was worth taking out a subscription to *The Leader* where each week you found recommended solutions to every crossword contest. Plenty of people did. At the height of its popularity, *The Leader* had a paid circulation of over 600,000.

You could even save yourself the bother of filling in each coupon. For a few shillings, a tipster would send you a duplicated leaflet explaining how to make out a form rather like a football coupon giving the required number of permutations of the alternative words you have selected.

If you were really lazy, all you need do was to send a postal order to Mrs. Hutt of Birmingham ('The winner of 89 crossword prizes in $2\frac{1}{2}$ years'). She supplied her own coupons, filled them in with guaranteed unduplicated solutions and submitted them in your name. Apart from the fee you paid her – about a shilling for each coupon – you were also required to give her one-fifth of your winnings if she came up trumps.

Although several journals have been published in the United States devoted entirely to crossword puzzles, no such enterprises seem to have got off the ground in Great Britain. A paper called *The Crossword Weekly* was delivered free to every home in Worthing, starting on November 8th, 1933. Crudely printed in green ink, it contained advertisements for local traders, household hints and news of local events. A 'Crossword for Men' offered twenty prizes of razors, blades and shaving sticks. A second crossword aimed at the ladies offered twenty pairs of artificial silk stockings. In this first issue the Editor bravely stated: 'Suggestions and criticisms are welcome at this office; we are not too old in the head to accept or consider well meant advice. It is our intention to improve as we go along (it takes years to grow an oak) so do not be too hard on us at first'. Sadly the oak never got beyond the sapling stage; the paper died within two years.

6. A Lifetime of Puzzles

In 1970, Simon and Schuster published Crossword Puzzle Book Number 100 – 'a cause for cerebration and celebration'. Like the previous ninety-nine, it was edited by Margaret Petherbridge – or to be more accurate, Margaret Farrar. Miss Petherbridge married the publisher John Farrar in 1926.

Margaret, newly graduated from Smith College, got her first job in 1920 as secretary to John O'Hara Cosgrave, editor of the magazine section of the New York *World*. One of her jobs was to see that the puzzles appeared without typographical errors. To the distress of Mr. Cosgrave, public attention was always drawn to these errors by 'F.P.A.' in that popular columnist's part of the paper. Margaret was given the job for much the same reason that a cub reporter is expected to write up the local dog shows – everyone else despised the job. She became so adept at stopping errors that she soon became the unofficial crossword editor.

In 1924 with Prosper Buranelli and Gregory Hartswick, she compiled the first Crossword Puzzle Book. Hartswick, by the way, stayed with the *World* puzzles until his death in 1948; Buranelli left the team in 1930 to join the news commentator Lowell Thomas.

One of Margaret's tasks was to reply to the hundreds of letters she received from fans. To a journalist from the *American Magazine* in 1925 she commented that some of them were so illiterate that she wondered how in the world their writers could solve a verbal puzzle. Through most of the letters ran a note of humorous resentment. Resentment toward puzzle publishers for putting temptation in their way; resentment toward themselves

The First Lady of Crosswords: Margaret Petherbridge Farrar

because they couldn't resist the temptation. When she wrote to the playwright and novelist Booth Tarkington asking him to construct a puzzle to appear in a book composed entirely by celebrities, she received the answer:

My dear Miss Petherbridge:

I have had trouble enough with your two books; and if I were able to build a cross-word puzzle, I am too kind-hearted to do it.

An enemy of mine sent me the first book just as I was about to do some overdue work. Then, two weeks later, when I had just finished your first book, he sent me the second, though I had written him, begging him not to do it.

When I get finished, I hope never to hear anything more about puzzles of any kind.

Malignantly yours,
BOOTH TARKINGTON.

One letter came to her from a rabbi who also enclosed a cross-word of his own invention:

Although I am guilty of having constructed the enclosed puzzle, I loudly proclaim that I am not a puzzle fan. On the contrary, I am ready to start a movement to have an amendment made to the Constitution, prohibiting the manufacture, sale, and distribution of all such pernicious articles. In the past year, they have slowed up the efficiency of this nation between 17 and 46 per cent. . . . I trust I am not an alarmist. But this craze has really gone too far. I can't go down the street here without being held up by someone who ought to be at home banging on his typewriter, or by some woman who ought to be mending her husband's socks, and asked what is a seven-letter word for Eskimo gefilte fish, or the like. . . . And the worst of it is that five quarters of the time I can give the pestiferous fans no answer.

Even though I did go for years to grammar school and theological seminaries, I really don't know even the first syllable of the two-letter word for an extinct New Zealand roach or a defunct South Persian seneschal. I simply don't.

The result is that I'm beginning to get an unenviable

reputation among our cognoscenti for something very close to illiteracy. They call me a 'Dumb Daniel' and a cretin. To my face they call me such names! What they say behind my back only an expert psychopathologist could understand.

I submit to you that it isn't right and proper. It just isn't. The first thing you know, the disappointed fans around here will be writing to the colleges from which I was not expelled to find out just how I managed to get by.

So I earnestly request that you print my puzzle, and announce that I don't care to be used as an information bureau by any fan, anywhere, at any time, until he, she, or it can make affidavit that he, she, or it has worked out every word in my poser.

If peace does not come to me even then, I threaten to construct a puzzle containing over a hundred poly-syllabic words, all taken from Bantu slang and obsolete Coptic! Maybe that will hold 'em.

In the spirit of silent martyrdom,

Yours,

LEWIS BROWNE.

After her marriage, Mrs. Farrar gave up the newspaper work and limited herself to editing the Simon and Schuster books which appeared at the rate of two a year. Then in February 1942, the *New York Times* decided to start a Sunday puzzle and asked her to be editor. The *New York Times* was the last major paper in America to adopt a crossword; not until September 1950, did it allow space for a daily puzzle. Mrs. Farrar retired from the paper in 1969.

During her time on the paper she regularly accepted puzzles from a high-school principal, an actress, an advertising man, three freighter captains, an Army corporal and a fourteen-year-old schoolboy. A good many came from inmates of prisons, who presumably have plenty of time on their hands. (A lifer at the Ohio State Penitentiary sold 250 puzzles to the newspapers in 1965 – at the rate of $10 for daily papers and $25 for Sunday papers.)

Mrs. Farrar has her own set of requirements for an acceptable puzzle. First, it must be what is called an over-all interlock – in other words every part of the puzzle is connected with every other part, allowing no unkeyed letters at all. Black squares are to be kept down to about one sixth of the total number of squares. Two-letter words are disallowed and a low word-count is aimed for, since the longer the words, the harder the puzzle.

Like all modern compilers, she avoids as far as possible such clichés as 'gnu' and 'proa'.

Occasionally, in her *New York Times* days, she received anguished calls for help. A student at Columbia University phoned in to tell her that a prerequisite for admission to a particular campus fraternity was to successfully complete the day's puzzle. Could she help? Realising that there was an ethical question involved, she threw him a few hints and kept her fingers crossed.

Then she received a call from a lovesick lass asking for a few hints on next Sunday's puzzle to impress her boyfriend who was an expert at crosswords. Reluctantly she divulged several words and hoped that she hadn't saddled some bright boy with a dumb girl for life.

Her rare errors have been eagerly seized on by her solvers. Her answer to the clue 'To succeed' was printed next day: 'To make a go of'. Of course, spaces between words disappear in a crossword, so she was dismayed to hear from a reader in the next post: 'What do you mean? Make a goof means succeed? You made a goof that time'.

On a celebrated occasion she received an indignant letter about her clue 'Manager of the Globe Theatre'. The writer had phoned New York's Globe to discover that the theatre had two managers and that neither of the names would fit. She had to break it to him gently that the chap she had in mind was called William Shakespeare.

Perhaps the most remarkable mistake was the one she related to an interviewer from the *New Yorker*: 'Not long ago a constructor sent in a puzzle that asked for Long John Silver's distinguishing characteristic, in nine letters. The answer, of course, was "wooden leg". Well, we'd just used Long John Silver in a puzzle, so I switched it to Captain Ahab's distinguishing characteristic. After the puzzle came out, I got a letter from an eight-year-old boy complaining that while he'd found that the only answer that fitted was "wooden leg", as a reader of "Moby Dick" he knew that Captain Ahab had an ivory leg. Perfectly true, but I couldn't help wondering, rather testily, what an eight-year-old was doing reading "Moby Dick"!'

7. The World's Most Famous Crossword

The Times held out as long as it could. No-one expected that London's most dignified newspaper would lend its space to what might turn out to be just a passing whim. But, as was shown in later years when *The Times* dared to print news on its front page, even the most venerable of institutions can bend to the winds of change. The Editor may have wondered what he was starting when, on January 16th, 1930, he printed a letter from Lieut. Commander A. C. Powell, R.N., who pointed out that *The Times* had been running a crossword puzzle in its Weekly Edition. 'Why not reproduce it in the daily edition?' the sailor suggested.

Two days later, *The Times* noted that many letters had been received. Five were printed as examples. His Honour Judge Sewell Cooper expressed the wish to see a *Times* crossword, while the only letter in opposition came from a Mr. Miller who cried: 'Let me entreat you to keep *The Times* free from puzzles of all sorts. Space there is precious and prestige also.' Two days later, the Editor referred to the continued response. Five more letters were given space in the columns; once again, the ratio was four in favour, one against. One of the readers looking forward to the idea was a descendant of one of *The Times*' original sixteen shareholders. Next day, there were five letters for, two against. One who didn't like the proposition wrote: 'I am a young woman and do not dislike all innovations; but I hate to see a great newspaper pandering to the modern craze for passing the time in all kinds of stupid ways.' But the majority had their way. On January 22nd, with more letters favouring a crossword puzzle

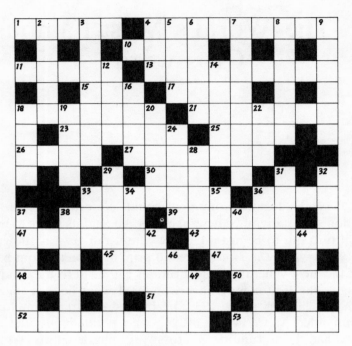

PUZZLE No. 11

Times *crossword number one*

ACROSS

1. Spread unevenly.
4. Part of a Milton title.
10. A month, nothing more, in Ireland.
11. He won't settle down.
13. 22 down should be this.
15. Cotton onto, so to speak.
17. Head of a chapter.
18. Denizen of the ultimate ditch.
21. Frequently under observation.
23. What's in this stands out.
25. Flighty word.
26. If the end of this gets in the way the whole may result.
27. Retunes (anag.).
30. This means study.
33. Simply enormous.
36. There's a lot in this voice.
38. This elephant has lost his head.
39. A turn for the worse.
41. Done with a coarse file.
43. Red loam (anag.)
45. This rodent's going back.
47. Makes a plaything with its past.
48. Wants confidence.
50. A mixed welcome means getting the bird.
51. This girl seems to be eating backwards.
52. The men in the moon.
53. A pinch of sand will make it dry.

58

2. Heraldic gold between mother and me.
3. Out of countenance.
4. Upset this value and get a sharp reproof.
5. Intently watched.
6. In some hands the things become trumpets.
7. A religious service.
8. This horseman has dropped an h.
9. Sounds like a curious song.
12. This ought to be square.
14. Momentary stoppage.
16. Written briefly.
18. Calverley's picturesque scholars carved their names on every one.
19. Site of 45 across.
20. Precedes advantage.
22. Parents in a negative way.
24. Used to be somewhere in France.
28. Happen afterwards.
29. Climbing instinct in man.
31. A terrestrial glider.
32. The final crack.
33. The little devil's on our money.
34. Simplest creature.
35. Time measurements.
36. Jollier than 4 across.
37. Ladies in promising mood.
38. Presents are commonly this.
40. Gets the boot.
42. Hail in Scotland may mean tears.
44. Works, but usually plays.
46. She's dead.
49. Only a contortionist could do this on a chair.

still being printed, the paper announced that its first weekly crossword would appear the next day.

The revolution in Printing House Square appears to have caused some concern down the road at Fleet Street for the *Daily Telegraph* rushed to prepare a large display advertisement in time to appear in *The Times* on the day after the first crossword appeared.

ARE YOU A CROSSWORD ENTHUSIAST?

Then take out your pencil and try the Daily Telegraph Crossword Puzzle reproduced below. You will discover a new world of pleasure in working out the ingenious clues, and further, you will be delighted to know that these famous puzzles are *A Regular* Daily *Feature of the Daily Telegraph.*

Needless to say, *The Times* wasn't going to stand for that! In the same issue as this hopeful advertisement, it informed the world that a series of daily puzzles would commence in *The Times* on February 1st.

The shock waves of this momentous event were felt even

across the Atlantic, where an amazed New York *Evening Post* broke the news to its readers. The American paper reprinted the puzzle and commented that the clues were 'rather easy' although it didn't attempt to supply any answers. The New York correspondent of *The Times* wired back to London that a veteran American puzzlist had solved it in one and a quarter hours. The *Evening Post*'s own crossword, on the other hand, had taken him all of seven minutes.

Not until 1970 was the identity revealed of the compiler of the first crossword in *The Times*. Faced with the problem of finding a puzzle constructor, Mr. Barrington-Ward (later Editor of the paper) had asked his close friend, Robert Bell of *The Observer*, for advice. Bell in turn asked his son, Adrian, to produce a crossword. Adrian was then 28 years old, had written one book and had been farming in Suffolk for ten years. But he had never compiled a crossword before – in fact, he'd never even solved one! 'You have ten days to learn', his father informed him. Forty years later, he was still compiling crosswords for *The Times*, including *Times Crossword No. 10,000*. In a 1970 interview published in the paper, Adrian Bell recalled that at first he submitted two puzzles a week at three guineas each; later he produced four a week. This effort wore out one dictionary every year. Occasionally he slipped in farming words and worried in case it wasn't fair. He had admitted to spelling Rossetti incorrectly in one puzzle because he had no facilities in his study for checking it – and remembers another discomfiture created by an error in the *Oxford Dictionary of Quotations*. 'I think you must be near dotty to spend your life setting crosswords', is how he has summed up his career.

The Times puzzle was warmly received. On the occasion of the hundredth puzzle, a gratified reader wrote in to claim that he had solved all the puzzles so far and had found only one word unknown to his wife and himself – 'cantrip'. He admitted, though, that some clues didn't yield their secret until midnight. Much more boastful was the man who penned a letter to the Editor with the information that he answered the clues without referring to the grid – in other words, without drawing any help from the letters supplied by interlocking words.

Proof of the puzzle's hold over the Establishment came during the 1930 Lambeth Conference when a Bishop, surrounded by copies of *The Times*, wearily asked another cleric: 'Do you think you could find me a copy in which the crossword puzzle has not been solved?' Rumour even had it that the Chairman of the Conference was surreptitiously grappling with the clues while the speeches were in progress. Some while later, another Reverend, observing the clue 'Home of the fatted calf now a days' (Gaiter), wrote to the paper suggesting episcopal authorship of the puzzles.

Guessing the identity of the compiler soon became an obsession with readers. Norman and Edith Campbell offered this analysis: 'Some of your composers (your anagram fiend, for instance) are not self-revealing; but one of them has told us so much about himself through his clues that we have come to feel for him an affectionate interest. He is a man between 55 and 60, educated at Eton and Oxford. In his youth he read for the Bar, but does not now practise the law or any other of the chief professions. Yet he is not a squire or a businessman. We have sometimes suspected that he is the secretary of an organisation connected (but not very directly) with the stage. He has no young children (or what would be more likely) grandchildren; he may even be a bachelor, for his interest in women seems to be confined to their hair. Modern literature does not appeal to him; but he is well read in the English classics and particularly the nineteenth-century poets. Though he is generally well-informed, his knowledge has some extraordinary gaps; he knows nothing of geography or of the works of Mr. Belloc (how otherwise could he place the Llama in the East?). In sport, cricket is his main pleasure, but he plays a little golf and billiards; he does not hunt and seldom shoots; his travels do not take him off the beaten track. Occasionally, we get glimpses of passing incidents in his career. Thus we were sorry when his *Chambers Dictionary* wore out and was replaced by a *Concise Oxford*; we rejoiced when he lately took a holiday in the North and discovered the joys of high tea. But since we have not kept a diary for him, we have forgotten many of these details; perhaps other of his regular clients can amplify our sketch.'

Further deductions came a few days later from another reader whose detective work has indicated that the compiler was either a clergyman or had been bred in a mid-Victorian rectory, had read Hamlet for his School Certificate, had acquired a taste for Tennyson, Clough and Spenser while up at Oxford. Thereafter, the compiler had lived in London where he suffered greatly from barrel organs and had now retired to the country. Furthermore, he had a son or a brother in India and a daughter in revolt.

Admiral Jackson, however, voiced his opinion that the puzzles were the work of several people, including at least one woman. Allan Baird, of Redhill, offered a few rebuttals to some of the earlier conclusions when he pointed out that the framer of puzzles had located Siberia in Europe (which not even an Old Etonian would do) and not long afterwards had referred to bottomry as a form of insurance, which no barrister should do. Again, 'prone' was given as 'back to the land', the author being apparently unaware that when prone, it is not the back which is next to the land. Only recently has *The Times* revealed that its crosswords are the creations of a group of compilers.

By 1933, *The Times* had celebrated its thousandth puzzle, an event which stimulated one reader to put pen to paper:

> The Thousandth! Or, as you would call it, 'M', Sir;
> Is't possible our brains in wordy wars
> (Though not perhaps designed to fire the Thames, Sir)
> Ten hundred times have matched themselves with yours!
>
> A thousand bouts of (anag.) transformations,
> Of cunning lures, clipped, hidden, punned, reversed,
> Have claimed their hours in each day's occupations
> And even robbed our sleep, with wiles accurst.
>
> Well, life Crosswordless would be much forlorner,
> And we've a thousand hours to thank you for,
> Praying that, in that bottom right-hand corner
> You'll go on giving us a thousand more!

On the same day the Editor of *The Times* gave a variety of quotes (Duke of Gloucester: 'I moralise two meanings in one word') in support of his theory that the Bard was familiar with crosswords, then surmised that the origin of the puzzle lay in the ancient East. 'It is difficult to imagine any reason why cadi, effendi, muezzin, vizier and such words should ever have been invented except to get crossword composers out of trouble. Scheherazade, most probably, never knew the gnu, but there are even stranger beats, and from her harem she must have heard the dziggetai, the wild ass (or was it the onager?) stamping o'er Bahram's head while he lay fast asleep. Better evidence still, Ur, that ancient place which may be called the patron city of crosswords, lay not too far away, and Iraq – the unique, Q ending Iraq – was on her doorstep. So it can be assumed that she was surrounded by most of the essential ingredients of the crossword.'

Geoffrey Ellinger added further evidence a few days later as backing for the Shakespeare hypothesis. 'What argument is needed when we can turn to the First Quarto of Hamlet and read that Polonius, discussing with Ophelia, Hamlet's curious behaviour, asks her "Have you sent him any crosse words of late?" This suggests at once that Shakespeare not only knew crosswords but disliked them, for he seems to imply that they can be counted as a cause of insanity. Scoffers may argue that the passage is not genuine as it does not occur in the First Folio. Let them scoff. It is plain enough the Shakespeare of Hamlet was an inexpert, a disgruntled solver. When he came to revise the play, he had learnt wisdom. He was no longer a hater of crosswords but an ardent and successful solver. Absurd to suggest that they can cause madness! Out goes the offending paragraph, and crosse words do not appear in the Folio Hamlet!'

From time to time *The Times* has been pleased to print congratulatory letters from its readers. One claimed that the crossword was just what the doctor ordered. When his wife was suffering from shock as the result of a fall, her physician had prescribed her to complete *The Times* crossword every day. From Mysore Province in South India, a thank you letter said that the value of the puzzle was increased a thousandfold in replacing theatres and cinemas where these luxuries were unobtainable. But the crossword was a 'very evil and corrupting influence' according to a reader in Bangkok. He received his copies of the paper in batches of six. Determined to do each crossword strictly in turn, he was in the habit of turning to the first full of hope and endeavour. Eventually, he would be forced to cheat and look up the answer in the next day's solution. Reminding the Editor that nothing is more despicable than the man who cheats himself, he sadly admitted 'I realise the futility of trying to excuse myself by sneaky little thoughts that I should, of course, have tumbled to it presently if only I had gone on thinking a little longer.'

More confident in his own ability was the reader who wrote in 1933 to boast that he had correctly solved all the 1,272 puzzles so far. An extensive correspondence was started the following year by Sir Josiah Stamp, Director of the Bank of England, who bragged that after only one week's acquaintance with *The Times* crossword, he had solved it in fifty minutes – with the assistance of his family, however. Nobel Peace Prize Winner, Sir Austen Chamberlain, clocked in a few days later at forty-one minutes and added that the Provost of Eton was accustomed to time his egg by the puzzle. And he didn't like hard-boiled eggs!

A claim of fourteen minutes came from another reader – performed under the worst of conditions, too. He did it in a railway tea room, with a bad stye in one eye and having just returned from a long and *Times*-less holiday so that he was out of training. The Editor then printed a long list of times submitted by correspondents ranging from the 12 minutes 59 4/5 seconds of Lord Russell of Killowen to the 49 minutes of Major-General Sir Louis Jackson. One 79-year-old did it unaided in one hour.

The recreational value of the puzzle to commuters was outlined by one reader who vaunted that he completed it between two stations, $3\frac{1}{2}$ minutes apart. 'The team spirit is essential,' wrote one traveller who usually finished it within a nine mile stretch of his daily express journey. His record was a mere five miles. 'The team consists of three. There are (a) the centre-forward; (b) the outside-right, who is an expert in modern literature, anagrams and farming terms; and (c) the outside left, who is only included for the remains of a classical education and because he buys the paper. We could do with a centre-forward who can recite the whole of Shakespeare.' The writer, who boarded the train each morning at Shenfield, signed himself

'Yours, 8.4. a.m.'.

A welcome counterbalance to these bombasts came with a sad note from one puzzler who had solved the puzzle correctly only once. That historic occasion took one day, seven hours and fourteen minutes. A subsequent claim came from one reader who took forty hours.

P. G. Wodehouse lamented: 'To a man who has been beating his head against the wall for twenty minutes over a simple anagram, it is gall and wormwood to read a statement like that one about the Provost of Eton and the eggs. May I commend your public spirit in putting the good old emu back into circulation as you did a few days ago! Now that the Sun-God Ra has apparently retired from active work, we are intensely grateful for an occasional emu.'

Another eminent man of letters, E. V. Lucas, regretted that he rarely finished one at all and never on the same day. A Yorkshire-man took inspiration from the Provost of Eton: 'I had hoped from Sir Austen's letter that boiling an egg might help. I started at 8.00 and it is is now 15.05 and the egg has burst.'

Not everyone was willing to believe the tall talk of the successful solvers. 'Let *The Times* take a public hall and gather together all these wonderful men and give them a crossword each. No one to leave the hall unless he has solved it. A start might be made at 10 a.m. and I suggest that the Provost of Eton might be allowed to bring his cooking apparatus, as they would all appreciate an egg about 2 p.m.'

A note of frustration came from a politician: 'There was a puzzle a little while ago which I abandoned because of one baffling word of six letters. The clue was "political horse-power". I spurred my mind as hard as I could, but it refused to provide a useful suggestion. On the next morning, while I was still half asleep, I turned at once to the answer, and I cannot say whether I was more annoyed or flattered to find that it was a kindly allusion to

Yours faithfully
Edward Shanks'.

At least he could take consolation from the lady of 70 who had just done the crossword without getting a single word right.

One of the odd events that add colour to the world of the crossword took place in 1935 when a lady reader struggled with a clue for a four-letter word, 'Indian who follows St. Katherine in London'. She wondered if this was a reference to the church in which a thanksgiving sermon is given every year in memory of a former Lord Mayor who narrowly escaped being killed by a lion while travelling in Africa. Seeking confirmation of the name of the church, she asked her flatmate who was reading another section of *The Times*. 'That's right,' was the reply. 'There's an announcement here that the 286th Lion Service will be held tomorrow at St. Katherine Cree Church.' Complete coincidence, as the compiler had no fore-knowledge of when his puzzle would be printed.

Rarely is *The Times* caught out by a reader alert to a piece of slipshod clue-writing. It is an accepted rule that any clue should yield only one possible correct answer. The clue 'Six consonants and the letter "a" five times' fell short of this ideal, admonished one correspondent. The solution given the next day was 'Panama Canal'. However, the indignant puzzler had been torn between 'Kanaka Pagan', 'Bahama Macaw', 'Malaga Cabal', and those two delightful melodies, 'Sahara Sarah' and 'Havana Madam'. An even more elegant possibility was offered by another reader who suggested 'Abracadabra'.

A worse pitfall was perpetrated by the compiler who gave 'The domineering horseman should see a blacksmith' as the clue for 'riding roughshod'. As a blacksmith was quick to point out, the man who rides roughshod over anyone must have only just come from the blacksmith's. The farrier has roughed the horse by inserting two spiked nails into the heels of the shoes to prevent slipping on icy roads. These nails wear down quickly and have to be constantly removed. The countryman who originated the expression knew that to be ridden down at all was unpleasant enough – to be ridden down by a freshly roughed horse was even more unpleasant.

The paper's biggest clanger was dropped in 1938 when a line of Wordsworth was made to read 'A Pagan nourished in a creed outworn'. The third word should have been 'suckled'. A stream of letters landed on the Editor's desk . . . some courteous, some

66

angry, some in verse. The most painful were those that voiced
sarcasm at what was assumed to be the compiler's prudery in
shielding his readers from the poet's own homely word. An
apology on the leader page gave the defence that the puzzle was
now nine years old and this was the first time that a howler had
run through a complete edition. However, 'nearly every letter
revealed much of the mind of its writer, that the blunder was
almost worth making.'

Readers of *The Times*, faced with such magnificent clues as
'The bunippedd' (solution: 'Nipped in the bud') must thank their
lucky stars that they don't live in New York. When W. H. Auden
left there in 1972 to take up residence in Oxford, he remarked:
'I must say the crossword in the *New York Times* frequently
drives me up the wall with rage because of the lack of precision
in its clues. The clues in British crosswords may be more com-
plicated but they are always fair. For example: "Song goes dry
for a ruined dean".' While this clue might baffle Americans,
Auden explains how simple it is: ' "Dry" is "sere". If you ruin
the word "dean" by spelling it backwards, you get "naed".
Putting them together produces "serenade". Why don't people
use their heads?'

One who has a higher opinion of the *New York Times* crossword is Bob Schwartz, the man who designed the first atomic
artillery shell. When asked how he felt when it first exploded, he
answered: 'It's the feeling you get when you've completed one of
the more difficult puzzles in the *New York Times*.'

The fact that there are no major differences in style between
the first 1930 puzzles in *The Times* and today's crosswords suggests that readers are more than satisfied with them. One reader
suggested a possible improvement when he wrote in 1958
requesting a small change in the layout. He wished the paper to
add by each puzzle the phrase: 'Warning. Confidential. Clues
and answers should not be discussed in public'. There was a
sensible reason behind the request. Every morning on the train a
group of gamesmen did the puzzle in concert and in loud voices,
depriving the writer and other travellers of the satisfaction of
doing it single-handed. This prompted a second reader to express
the glow of self-satisfaction he enjoyed when he heard fellow

commuters discussing a clue he had already solved. At the same time, he added, advice on a difficult clue is always welcome.

'Your two correspondents seem to have overlooked the true value of the crossword,' chided a third reader. 'Those who, like myself, invariably complete the puzzle in less than ten minutes don't just sit back in smug self-satisfaction when they see others in despair. No, we hold up our puzzle, completed in ink, and in order to give a show of indifference, we study long and earnestly all the advertisements on page one, all the while hoping that those poor fish are marvelling at our superiority and are surreptitiously trying to cheat. I feel sure, Sir, that this knowledge will encourage advertisers to make even more use of your front page. When, as inevitably happens, we are defeated by some very obscure quotations or by a misprint (there have only been three), we fake the answer in letters sufficiently shaky to be illegible, though we have the sneaking fear that some bold spirit will ask us what the word really is.'

The ability to tackle crosswords in *The Times* has been cited in the High Court as a measure of the power of intellect. In 1958 a witness testified that he and another man used to compare their solutions to the crossword. 'He had nearly always completed it and I hadn't.' Counsel took pains to remind His Lordship that 'there are stupid people who do it very easily and professors of the Royal Society who cannot do it at all.'

Some measure of the high intellect of *Times* readers was given in 1970 when the paper organised its first annual Crossword Championship in association with the distillers of *Cutty Sark* whisky. The contest was open to anyone sending a fully correct solution to any one of five puzzles appearing during May. To the Editor's astonishment, over twenty thousand readers qualified! The number was reduced by a series of elimination puzzles. One thousand got the first one right – the principal failure being unfamiliarity with the word 'uffish' from poem relating to Jabberwocky. Only 302 passed the next stage – an unusually difficult puzzle. One of the answers, 'amenta' (catkins), was ·yielded by the clue 'They hang from the trees in the book of Jeremiah.' Frantic competitors scoured the book of Jeremiah, not noticing the *Lamenta*tions of Jeremiah in which the answer lay hidden.

The second eliminator was so difficult that only 42 correct solutions were sent in, so all 302 were invited to the two-day finals at the Europa Hotel. On the first day, eight puzzles were set, with a maximum of half an hour allowed for each. Bonus points were given for speed. The following day, 36 semi-finalists were required to solve four more puzzles. Champion crossworder was Roy Dean, 43, a Foreign Office diplomat. He had recently returned from a ten year stint in Ceylon during which time he had never seen *The Times* crossword. Roy reported that he normally managed to complete the puzzle during his 17-minute train journey into London. He won the Championship by one point, scoring 375, only one short of the possible maximum. His one error? For 'reflection familiar to polar explorers' he gave 'ice-brick' instead of 'ice-blink'.

Roy didn't even realise at the half-way stage that he was one of the leaders – he left the hotel before the placings were announced. Fortunately he ignored his wife's advice not to waste the train fare back to London the following day. 'I was flabbergasted. I did not think I had much chance against the best crossword brains in Britain. I like crosswords because they are fun, and because the compiler can test the solver's range of knowledge. You have to be not so much well educated as well read.'

Among the 39 semi-finalists were ten women, including two teachers from Benenden Girls School who raced each other daily to complete *The Times* crossword. Another semi-finalist was no less than the Arundel Herald Extraordinary. Contestants eliminated on the first day included Alvar Lidell, the news reader, and Tom Driberg, M.P.

The 1971 Championship was won by 1970's runner-up, James Atkins. James, a professional singer and singing instructor, had previously won a nationwide crossword contest organised by the *Daily Express* in the 1950's. He completed the final four puzzles – one of them designed to be particularly difficult – with no mistakes in an average time of eleven minutes. The runner-up, a schoolmaster, also achieved all-correct results in an average time of twenty minutes. James Atkins described the qualities needed to become crossword champion as 'practice and a ragbag of a

Silver trophy awarded to the winner of the first National Crossword Championship sponsored by Cutty Sark Scotch Whisky and The Times.

mind that stores away completely unrelated bits of fact'. His greatest sense of achievement came from solving 'Dial 999 if upset – you might get him.' Answer: 'Beast'. (Look up the Revelation of St. John.)

The toughest piece of luck in the contest undoubtedly went to the Edinburgh puzzler who failed on only one clue: 'Dress for U.S. quarterdeck'. He weighed 'slip' against 'suit' and finally put down 'slip', hoping that the English quarterdeck was called a slipdeck in the American Navy. Sadly, he failed to spot that an American deck is also a pack of cards, a quarter of which is a suit!

The following year, the champion completed the four final puzzles in the amazing average time of $8\frac{1}{2}$ minutes. John Sykes explained that he usually turns to the crossword in *The Times* at 11 p.m. His best ever time is $3\frac{1}{2}$ minutes – the day after that he went down with pneumonia. Perhaps Mr. Sykes might be said to have had an unfair advantage over his fellow contestants . . . his occupation. He is the Editor of the Concise Oxford Dictionary.

To return to the question that has intrigued puzzlers for so long: 'Who writes the crosswords for *The Times*?'. Today's Crossword Editor is Edmund Akenhead, a retired solicitor. His team of ten compilers includes an author, a Brighton secretary, a member of the Magic Circle, and a major-general. Recently, Akenhead explained some of the rules that his compilers must stick to. First of all, they must work within the framework of one of the twenty-five standard grids used by the paper. No one word may have more 'blind' letters than 'open' ones. He is critical of many other puzzles where five-letter words with only two open are not uncommon.

Another *Times* requirement is that no word may begin with two blind letters. Elsewhere, there must never be more than two consecutive blind letters. Finally, all sections of the puzzle must communicate in such a way that no one section can be isolated by the blacking in of one more square. This prevents the type of design which has only one entrance into one section of the puzzle.

Akenhead's own favourite answer, revealed in *Daily Telegraph Weekend Magazine* interview by Anthony Grey, is HONORIFI-CABILITUDINITATIBUS. Meaning 'honourableness', the word appears in one of Shakespeare's plays. The Clue?
'   ' (27) (Love's Labour's Lost).

In recent years, Mr. Akenhead has noticed the emergence of a curious turn of events: the simultaneous and coincidental appearance of similar clues in different newspapers. On May 19th, 1972, the *Daily Telegraph* carried the clue: 'Harsh treatment for unseasoned timber' (3, 4). On the same day, *The Times* used the clue: 'What the purchaser of unseasoned timber gets'. The solution to both, of course, was the same: 'Raw deal'.

The following day, Mr. Akenhead remarked that he could not recall so close a coincidence in his six and a half years in the chair, but added: 'Experienced crossword minds are a particular type of agile, word-conjuring brain, and they do tend to think alike. Given "electricity bill" as an answer, the idea of writing the clue "charge of the light brigade" would very easily come to different compilers working quite independently – but it would be rejected because it has been used before.'

The Times took the opportunity to ask Miss M. R. K. Binstead, the *Telegraph*'s crossword editor for over fifteen years, for her comments. She agreed on the statistical probabilities of compilers writing similar clues but didn't think the coincidence was very remarkable: 'If two people had come up with closely similar clues for a difficult word like myxomatosis, I would have thought it was much more extraordinary.'

Seven days later, it happened again! The *Financial Times* had 'Parson operating on a lofty plane' while *The Times* had 'No hedge-hopping priest'. As *The Times* suggested the day after, you will not need a sky pilot to be inspired with the answer in 3 and 5.

Incidentally, readers of *The Times*' superb offspring, *The Times Literary Supplement*, may wonder why this journal doesn't feature a crossword. As a matter of fact, it used to run a regular crossword competition. However, when Stanley Morison took over as Editor, he got rid of it immediately. He even refused to publish the solution of the puzzle given in his predecessor's last number.

PUZZLE No. 12

'Reverses' – a specialist puzzle from The Times

ACROSS

1. Rev. of 33 (5).
4. Rev. of 32 (4).
6. Rev. of 31 (4).
10. Rev. of 30 (5).
11. Fruit, but fruit gone to waste (9).
12. 'How's that?' – 'Not out!' (6).
13. Emperor externally meek (7).
15. Globular disease? (6).
16. A profitable concern (8).
20. Acrobatic vessels (8).
22. Red Sea (anag.) (6)
25. In this London suburb there is not fire and slaughter, but there is almost the converse of it (7).
27. Mr. Jingle had it in common with the Great (6).
29. What makes Celia prim? This (9).
30. Rev. of 10 (5).
31. Rev. of 6 (4).
32. Rev. of 4 across (4).
33. Rev. of 1 across (5).

DOWN

1. Rev. of 28 (4).
2. Evidently not a brown study (9).
3. Morbid changes of tissue (7).
4. They go to and fro in the rain (6).
5. Embrocation (8).
7. Rev. of 26 (5).
8. Rev. of 25 down (5).
9. The Indian takes the pledge (6).
14. Rev. of 18 (4).
17. More likely to be dispatched than hatched (two words) (6, 3).
18. Rev. of 14 (4).
19. Samuel Butler frequently was (8).
21. Picture palace (6).
23. This doesn't lead to an engagement (7).
24. This man does not provide a high obstruction (6).
25. Rev. of 8 (5).
26. Rev. of 7 (5).
28. Rev. of 1 down (4).

73

PUZZLE No. 13

'Quotations' – another specialist crossword from The Times

N.B. – Unclued words form three well-known quotations from the plays of Shakespeare – Nos. 12, 21, 29, 1 down (10 words); 20, 8, 31 (five words); and 23, 6, 15 (five words).

ACROSS

1. Wild talk at court, in short makes part of the circle (8).
5. Not moving (6).
10. An inelegant sort of plant (9).
11. Lord who might well be named (5).
13. French philosopher – did he talk nonsense? (7)
17. Star of use to furniture removers (6).
19. They disturb the ladies (6).
24. Final verdict, generally used with cutting effect (7).
25. This creature is cut back by another (6).
28. The high note is first rate in the mountains (5).
30. Make a nominal entry (6).

DOWN

2. A small advertisement to a politician is without limit (two words) (2, 3).
3. Spitefulness (7).
4. This is certainly over-quick (4).
7. A game on a settled course proves musical (two words) (5, 4).
9. What he begs is not the 1 down (9).
14. Hope's path (anag.) (9).
16. When Christmas comes (9).
18. Of second quality (two words) (4, 4).
22. This suburb should prove a misnomer after 11.30 (7).
26. A scholar has a drink in France (5).
27. And the same scholar gets drunk in France (4).

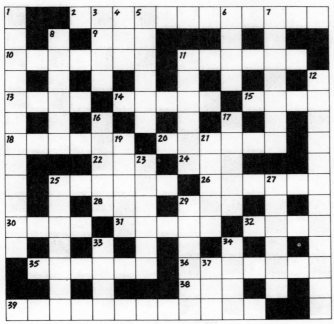

PUZZLE No. 14

'Anagrams' – another Times *specialist crossword, dating from the 1930's*

N.B. – Of the unclued words: 1 is an anagram of 8 followed by one of 25 across. 2 is an anagram of 26 followed by one of 35 across. 12 is an anagram of 18 followed by one of 11 across. 39 is an anagram of 5 followed by one of 29 down.

ACROSS

9. Both hard and soft (3).
10. Very fine they are (7).
13. Built a lighthouse with stone (4).
14. Fish alight (5).
15. Statesman cut short and consequently heated (4).
20. Jenny? (6).
22. 'The weary, way-worn wanderer'(—) (3).
24. Food for that infernal dog (3).
28. Easier to get into than out of (3).
29. Extremes of 17 (3).
30. A gasteropod, according to Frederick the Great (4).
31. Instrument of a festive turn (5).
32. Its content is superficial (4).
36. You get it to start with so put in it to start with (7).
38. It's a gift, as you might say (3).

DOWN

3. Spanner (4).
4. It goes on the line (3).
6. Not the one Brutus referred to in the affairs of men (4).
7. Presumably what cats are let out of (7).
11. Holiday dug-out (6).
16. This beast sounds as though he might come to the point (5).
17. 'I will', said Baroness Orczy (5).
19. A great diamond (5).
21. Sunny (5).
23. Takes legal possession (6).
25. His work is giving out (7).
27. It's a bit thick (6).
33. Stone horse (4).
34. Chilblain from a cycle of slang (4).
37. Horse-sense should teach him not to (3).

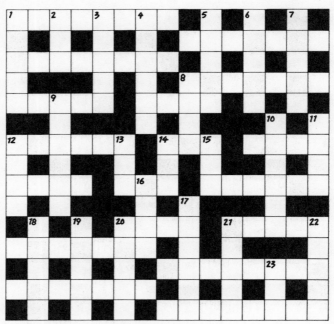

PUZZLE No. 15

'Green Study' – a Times crossword from 1935

Unfortunately, *The Times* has long since ceased to run these specialist crosswords.

ACROSS

All the words are associated with the word 'green'.

DOWN

1. The great brute puts a letter before the boss (5).
2. Folk song in Scotland (3).
3. Apostrophize a tree (5).
4. The official seems to incite Richard to err (6).
5. Tea taken with an orange (5).
6. Naval island (5).
7. Day economists look forward to (5).
8. Colour surprises come out of (4).
9. Equal legs give this crustacean its name (6).
10. The Asiatic takes an article to heart (6).
11. He is in and, for example, up (4).
12. Red bishop (4).
13. Clearly it goes far up (3).
14. This river is the Irishman's idea of 14 across (3).
15. A motor out of order (3).
16. One cannot say it is not in the least annoying (4).
17. A sunny element (6).
18. A range of note, as it were (5).
19. Fish on ice (5).
20. A singular science for boys (5).
21. The devotee seems a fraud (5).
22. Lots of entertainers (5).
23. The slippery part of banana peel (3).

8. The World's Toughest Puzzle Series

If *The Times* crossword puzzle is the world's most famous, then by common consent the world's toughest are those that have appeared weekly for almost fifty years in *The Observer*. Only *The Listener* can claim to rival this series for consistent ingenuity. This supremacy was won for *The Observer* first by the great Torquemada (Edward Powys Mathers) and then by his successors.

Mathers was born at Forest Hill in 1892, the only son of Edward Peter Mathers, the founder of the newspaper *South Africa*, and of Mary Powys, through whom he was related to the three Powys brothers, T. F., Llewelyn and John Cooper. In 1924, while earning his living as a literary critic, he came across the crossword puzzle which had then just reached England. At this time crosswords on both sides of the Atlantic employed only the simplest 'dictionary clues' but Mathers realised that with more difficult clues it held the makings of a first-class entertainment. While he may not have invented the 'cryptic clue', there is no doubt that he was the first compiler to use cryptic clues entirely. For the amusement of his friends, he constructed the first Torquemada puzzle, writing the clues in couplets, in the style then current in *The Observer*. Against his wishes, a friend took it to the Editors of the *Saturday Westminster*, who persuaded him to produce more. In all, Torquemada published twelve puzzles in this paper; their appearance was heralded by green posters bearing the warning 'Crosswords for Supermen'. Later the twelve were collected in a book entitled 'Crosswords for Riper Years'.

When the *Saturday Westminster* came to an end, Torquemada

was approached by *The Observer* to contribute puzzles on similar lines. The first was printed in March, 1926, and appeared under the title 'Feelers' as Mathers felt he was feeling his way with his new and wider public. Over the next few months he received a massive correspondence, much of it from readers protesting mildly that they were wasting many hours tussling with his clues. Within a couple of years he already had his copyists employing cryptic clues; at the same time his own 'constant solvers' were getting on his nerves and requesting a fuller display of his invention and ingenuity. He then abandoned the normal crossword grid pattern and devised a form without any black squares. This gave him greater elasticity in the choice of words and enabled him to reduce to a minimum the number of unchecked letters. Only his successor Ximenes had such mastery of the art of composing tortuous and exasperating – but always scrupulously fair – clues. During the years that he worked on *The Observer* puzzles, he received many letters from solvers indulging in speculations as to his identity. His fondness for Biblical clues led many to endow him with ecclesiastical rank. In fact, Edward Powys Mathers won considerable eminence under his own name as a poet and translator. Even the verse in which he composed his puzzles was often quite distinguished: one of his solvers wrote to say that she had learned many of his rhyme puzzles off by heart.

Enquiries were also frequent as to how he set about composing his weekly puzzles. Several years after his death, his widow answered this curiosity in the foreword to a book of Torquemada puzzles: 'I see him sitting cross-legged in bed, with a puzzle in front of him, looking very like a somewhat relaxed Buddha, a cigarette between his fingers and eyes fixed in the distance – until something clicks and, with a contented smile or discontented shrug, he writes on the list in front of him, and ticks off the word in gaily coloured chalk. Or prowling around his shelves in baggy flannel trousers, his shirt open at the neck and sleeves rolled above the elbow, in search of a quotation through which he would lead his solvers to read or reread some favourite in verse or prose. Or sitting at a table in the living room, kitchen or garden, one ankle resting on the other knee, a hand hugging the foot, drawing marginal decorations in vari-coloured chalks while he broods on some uninspiring word.'

How long did it take him to compile his masterpieces? According to his widow, the more straightforward puzzles took on average about two hours—although he rarely completed one at a sitting, preferring instead to divide into quarters and sandwich it with other work. Puzzles with the clues buried in a narrative story or those based on a particular book or author took longer because of the amount of preparation required. Although his remarkable fertility led many solvers to believe that a Torquemada team was at work, his only collaborator was his wife. Mathers would choose his subject and make a list of words he wished to include. His wife's part was to select from this list and construct the diagram. From time to time, readers would post him their own 'Revenge' puzzles and occasionally he would borrow a clue from one of these, but less than fifty of the thousands of clues he presented came from these contributions. When his widow examined some thirty thousand clues in *The Observer* series, she found the same word cropping up fifty times over the years and was astonished at how he succeeded in continually varying the clues.

Considering the difficulty of his puzzles, the wonder is that so many readers were able to solve them. Up to seven thousand correct solutions were received by *The Observer* each week, and it was estimated that another twenty thousand regularly completed the puzzle without bothering to put the result into the post in pursuit of the prizes for the first three correct solutions opened each week. However, on occasions there were only a handful of successful solvers—on at least two occasions the list of prize-winners was restricted to one lady. Torquemada addicts were widespread. Solutions were received from a man in West Africa who didn't even have a dictionary to turn to. The first air-mail post from India brought a solution, while another came from four men snowed up in Alaska with only a copy of *The Observer* for entertainment. A Scottish lady of over seventy relied on completing them before Morning Prayer, otherwise her worship was distracted. On the other hand, on one occasion the entire Balliol Common Room admitted that working in combine they still hadn't managed to finish one particularly braintwisting puzzle.

A great many solvers worked together in concert sometimes over the telephone: an anguished complaint came from a Scot bewailing the expenditure on trunk calls over one set of clues.

Up to his death in February, 1939, Mathers published 670 Torquemada puzzles in *The Observer*. It is a great pity that these have so long been out of print for so many years. A selection of 112 Torquemada puzzles was printed in book form in 1942 – *Torquemada: 112 Best Crossword Puzzles*, published by the Pushkin Press. More unusual is *The Torquemada Puzzle Book*, published by Victor Gollancz Limited in 1934. This contains a number of crossword puzzles with a Cheats' Dictionary containing a list of all the words used in the puzzles, but without definitions. *The Torquemada Puzzle Book* also includes a section of perforated tracing papers; the idea is that you can tear these out, lay them over the puzzle diagrams and work out your solutions. This way, the unmarked book can be enjoyed by more than one reader. The book finishes with a 100-page detective story called 'Cain's Jawbone'. What makes the story so special is that the pages are printed in the wrong order. Each page has been written so as to finish at the end of a sentence and readers were invited to work out the correct page sequence. Despite the offer of a cash prize, only three correct solutions were received by the publishers!

Mathers was succeeded by three compilers, one of whom was D. S. Macnutt – Senior Classics Master at Christ's Hospital School. In 1943 Macnutt adopted the pseudonym of 'Ximenes', the name of the Cardinal who followed the original Torquemada as leader of the Spanish Inquisition. Two years later, Ximenes took over the complete responsibility for crosswords in *The Observer*. One of Ximenes' introductions was the awarding of a regular prize to readers for compiling a cryptic clue to replace a straightforward definition clue given in his crossword.

Ximenes took the opportunity of confronting his solvers from time to time when he held Ximenes Dinners. A representative from *Time* magazine attended one of these at the Cafe Royal and marvelled at the reasoning behind some typical clues. For instance, the clue 'Pleased a bag £14 lighter' yielded the answer GLAD. The logical development of the answer: a glad-stone bag

CROSSWORD

A surrealist joke by David Tuhill, a graphic designer who teaches at the Royal College of Art

minus one stone (14 pounds).

'An important city in Czechoslovakia' turned out to be OSLO. No, you don't turn to your atlas to check it – just look closely at the middle of the word Czechoslovakia!

'Shortage of bats at a high level' gave the answer SANITY (i.e. not bats in the belfry).

Sporting a badge marked 'Mr X', Ximenes apologised to his dinner guests for one recent clue which had proved tougher than usual: 'Earnest money got by leaving deposit on old clothes'. The solution was DYEST. The cluemaster explained that deposits on old clothes referred to dye; to get money is to earn; earn out of earnest leaves -est.

Ximenes explained to the *Time* man that regular solvers take from two to four hours to complete the puzzle. Compiling them took him about one and a half hours. 'You have to be a lunatic with a distorted mind to do it.'

David Macnutt died early in 1972.

At the beginning of this Chapter I linked *The Listener* with *The Observer* as home of the most difficult crosswords on print. In truth, it's impossible to say which is the hardest. Mind you, in the beginning *The Listener* had good reason to print the most perplexing of puzzles – they were offering a prize for every correct solution sent to them. The paper, a BBC publication, employs an extensive number of compilers, all of whom hide under pseudonyms. The most influential of these puzzlers was the late Prebendary A. F. Ritchie, known to his readers as Afrit.

Among the many specialist types of crossword introduced in *The Listener* is the 'Knight's Move' variety, created by Cocos (D. H. S. Cox). In this the down clues are replaced by words which can make knight's moves, as in chess, instead of going straight down.

What can one say about *The Listener*'s puzzles except that week after week they never fail to display fiendish invention? Hundreds of new types of crossword have appeared there and to leaf through back numbers of the paper discovering them is a stimulating experience. The following selection was made at random by dipping into the files and gives only the merest impression of what Herculean tasks you will let yourself in for when you take my advice and take out a subscription.

PUZZLE No. 16

'The Gift Car' by Torquemada

The narrative type of crossword was almost certainly invented by Torquemada. This example dates from 1936.

I have always been used 39 rev. driving 2 40 & 6, and the 7 ac. at Brooklands will tell you all about my 15; but it was given a secondhand 27 25 rev. for Christmas, and 38 a rash moment after 24 rev. was prevailed upon to take out 20 43 and her little brother 45, without any preliminary 29.

She looked a nice little job of work (the 27 not 20) as I ran her out of the garage: her 1 dn. tyres were nearly new, she was upholstered in the most delicate of 21 & 6, and those hole arrangements at either side of the dashboard, for retaining one's 33 ac. of maps, cigarettes and apples had real 35 ac. Also her mascot, though actually, I 23 ac., the head of Mercury, impressively resembled a Burmese 32 with a 18 rev.

'Look, 36 dn.,' cried little 45, as he scrambled into the back seat and proceeded to kick the cushions with 30, 'there's 11 of room back here.' But 20 took no 12, preferring to sit in front with me. Bar the fact that I started in 3 and for a moment it looked as if we were returning, our progress for the first 25 rev. minutes was excellent; all those parts whose function it is to 10 proceeded to 10 with 13 rev.

It was only when we had reached the main road and I started to 33 dn. 5 it and 14 her up a bit, that I discovered, with no wish to look gift cars in the 7 dn., that she had more than one unworthy 42 rev.: 41, owing to some solution of continuity, she dropped 11 of 35 dn. rev. upon the place beneath; owing to excess of 1 ac., she rejoiced in the popular pastime of

83

Knock, Knock; owing, doubtless, to the presence of a 17 in the 23 dn. (as this leaves me); she emitted a horrible squeak; and these two sounds formed a 19 which did not 26 to her credit. Finally (and you will have to be as much of a 8 as I am to understand this), none of the wires were fancied by their own 36 ac., and consequently the 4 backed both ways.

Even so, the drive might have been a success had not a Foughastly errand-boy charged me from a right-hand side-street. Instinctively, to preserve his valuable bicycle, I charged the populous 34.

The consequent percussion 31 little 45 28 into 44 & 2 (see diagram 16). He came to earth I know not where. 20 and I took to our heels, while an incensed citizenry armed with 22 and using language, which ought to have been 9, proceeded to 37 hell out of the 27.

PUZZLE No. 17

'Knock Knock' – one of Torquemada's most famous crosswords

1	2	3	4	5	6	7	8	9	10	11	12	13
14						15			16			
17				18	19	20		21	22			
23		24		25					26	27		
	28				29		30				31	
32	33		34					35			36	
37					38	39		40				41
42		43	44	45		46				47	48	
49	50				51	52	53				54	
55								56				

N.B. – To save space, it must be imagined that each italic clue has been prefaced by the first player saying 'Knock-Knock,' the second saying 'Who's there?' and the first replying with a given-name. In the clue itself the second player asks 'Given-name who?' and the first player amplifies his previous answer, e.g., 'Ebenezer who?' 'Ebenezer black wood,' 'Eulalia who?' 'Eulalia nate my affections.' 'Cecilia who?' 'Cecilia game than I thought.'

ACROSS

1. 'Blank who?' 'Blank sitting down a minute?'
7. 'Blank who?' 'Blank 'd love to'.
14. 'Blank who?' 'Blank no-how'.
15 rev. Lear had a runcible one.
16. Mulde contributes to me.
17. It's awkward to find the Lord Chancellor upside down in the street on a rainy day.
19. Plant obtainable from high ground overlooking a river valley.
22 rev. A theocracy.
23. Wore a russet mantle in Shakespeare.
25. Out of the eater came forth meat.
26. 'Food for his . . ., repasture for his den'.
28. A peep into taste.
29. See 33.
30. 'Blank who?' 'Blank terrible state of affairs'.
31 rev. 54.
32. 'Blank who?' 'Blank fool and caught a cold'.
35. ⎫ 'Blank who?' 'Blank the bounds
42. ⎭ of possibility.
37. 'Blank who?' 'Blank out and do it again'.
39. Vowels of 53.
40. 'Blank who?' 'Blank by a tiger'.
44. ⎫
48. ⎭ Make a song about it.
46. 'Blank who?' 'Blank ute ickle sing'.
49. 'Blank who?' 'Blank, where is fancy bred?'
53. Creeper formed of Edmund and his son Charles.
55. 'Blank who?' 'Blank pants, I make-a you another pair'.
56 rev. Better in character than sugar.

DOWN

1. ⎫
9. ⎭ 'Blank who?' 'Blank a wireless?'
2 rev. Brownsea island is in this harbour.
3. ⎫
9. ⎭ 'Blank who?' 'Blank note of it'.
4. 'Blank who?' 'Blank attack of itch'.
6. 'Blank who?' 'Blank fool, aren't you?'
7. rev. ⎫ Volume of a particle of
5. ⎭ dust.
8. 'Blank who?' 'Blank I haven't had a drink all day'.
10. Room for a dislocated 25.
12. ⎫ 'Blank who?' 'Blank and a small
11. ⎭ stout'.
13. ⎫ 'Blank who?' 'Blank ropodist
9. ⎭ called about my corns?'
18. My small brother goes round the meadow.
20 rev. 27.
21. I'm in from the sign.
23 rev. 'Blank who?' 'Blanks pictures'.
24 rev. Impetus.
26. 'Blank who?' 'Blank mow the lawn'.
27. 'On Ararat there grew a vine; When . . . from her bathing rose'.
33. Gets into a 26 ac. with 29.
34. 'Blank who?' 'Blank ephant never forgets'.
36. With or may say without if you are slow to learn.
38. 'Blank who?' 'Blank who waits'.
39. My first is unchecked in 28, and my second in 13, 21, 23 dn., 52 and 55.
40. ⎫ 'Blank who?' 'Blank did me
52. ⎭ wrong'.
41. More than the reverse of negative colours.
43. '. . . dim . . . red, like God's own head'.
45 rev. There can be a chick before and a hen behind.
50. ⎫
47. ⎭ Almost poached rat.
51 rev. First half of 41.
52 rev. 39 do.
54 rev. 31.

85

PUZZLE No. 18

'Hell, said the Duchess' by Torquemada

N.B. – Words for which there are no clues will be found to build up a complete and delightful poem in four lines when arranged in the following order: 47, 1 *dn.*, 9, 16 *rev.*, 19, 49 *rev.*/36, 10, 44, 15, 45, 28 *ac.*/46, 1 *ac.*, 43, 31 *rev.*, 24/38, 8, 37, 5, 41, 7 *dn.*, (a), 7 *ac.*

ACROSS

12. This makes 11 clear.
13. The female 7 *dn.* becomes possessive, but continues to contain the male 8.
14. 44.
17 *rev.* It almost sounds as if this chaffinch had been thieved.
21 *rev.* Jerk of dogs at the beginning of scurvy.
23 *rev.* Sometimes I'm definitely cracked, and I'm never quite myself unless I'm locked up.
26. This goddess is a genus of carangoid fishes.
32. With the letter unchecked in 26, cruisers pass over me.
35, 34. My white bird and my minister are not large ones.
39. My first is unchecked in 6, and my second in 43.
40. Confusion! Turn the mats.
42. Tekoa's father made out of a rush.
48, 49. Out of a hundred trees indeed.

DOWN

2. Search for the editor of the Examiner.
3. My first is unchecked in 47 and my second in 48.
4. A hog can be one of us; we help you up; we bring you down.
6. No god, but an Ibsen girl.
11. See 12 and play with 10.
18. Whether well or ill, I'm found at the beginning of Debrett.
22 *rev.* Butcher-birds hie unchecked.
25. Matthew's dill.
27. Tepid Christian name of Ben Hur's author.
28. Stick stick should suggest.
29. 42 *dn.* might think this surgeon moist.
30 *rev.* 42 *dn.'s* verb ending.
33. A hut in the middle of a waterfall.
37. 20.
42. Father of a multitude in little.
44. My first is unchecked in 22 and my second in 19.

PUZZLE No. 19

'So Be It' by Torquemada

This crossword appeared in *The Observer* on New Year's Day, 1939 – shortly before Torquemada's death.

N.B. – Unclued words, when arranged in the following order, form Torquemada's hopeful quatrain for the day: 36 rev., 15, 45, 30 rev., 19, 49 rev., 1 ac., 48 rev., /4, 44, 22 rev., 4, 34 ac., 10, 34 dn., /43, 38, 13 rev., 7 ac., 1 dn., 49 rev., 28 rev., 43, 41 rev., /43, 8, 34 ac., 10, 5.

ACROSS

12 rev. Virginia President holds the clue.
14. See 29.
16. I ran into a rajah's trouble.
17. 'The . . . stands up, the keeper Stands up to keep the . . .'
19. A steward could not.
20. Roves around with 6, but is straight with 39.
21. Somewhat terminating.
24. 47.
25 rev. Allure in spite of having a very cold tail.
27 rev. Concern of Pharisees and Southern colonels.
29 rev. Revolutionary mood with 14.
33 rev. The English prevented 16 from visting me untimely.
39. See 20.
42 rev. If Aunt D replaced her 51 she might provide a clue.
50 rev. 15.
51. See 42 ac.

DOWN

2 rev. The Automobile Association causes a taxi accident.
3. Try your weight.
6. See 20.
7. ⎱ I file in a state of confusion
9. ⎰ through the quadrangle.
11 rev. Put silk shirt on horse?
21. My first two are unchecked in 5, and my third in 34 ac.
23. I wrote: 'Still are thy pleasant voices, thy nightingales, awake'.
26 rev. This plait would be a real ornament to the hair if there were nine.
31. ⎱ Nut-hatches sound an easy
32. ⎰ catch.
35. Borrowed a bit of preface to tile a closet.
37 rev. Bean of mixed letters.
40 rev. The man's a huzzy.
42 rev. 'Where doomsday may thunder and lighten And little 'twill matter to . . .'.
46 rev. 12 rev. has an expressive head.
47. 24.

87

The crossword grid (cells numbered):

Row 1: 1 2 3 4 5 6 7 8 9 10 11 12 13 14
Row 2: 15 · 16 · · · · · · · 17
Row 3: 18 · 19 20 · 21 · · · 22 · 23
Row 4: 24 25 · · · · 26 · · 27
Row 5: 28 · 29 · · 30 31 32 · · · · 33
Row 6: 34 · 35 · · 36 37 · · 38 39
Row 7: 40 41 · 42 · · 43 44 45 · · 46
Row 8: 47 · · 48 49 · 50 · · · 51 52 53
Row 9: 54 · · 55 · · 56 · · 57 58
Row 10: 59 · 60 · · · 61 · · · 62 · 63
Row 11: 64 · · · · · 65

PUZZLE No. 20

'Dancing Partners' by Torquemada

N.B. – The unclued words consist of nine groups of three, each group having the same initial and containing, straight or reversed, a man and a woman and the dance they danced together at the great Elysian ball. Two of the groups will be found to have the same initial, and in this case, of course, the solver can please himself as to who dances what with whom. Two words are bracketed, 20 *dn.* and 21, and 50 *dn.* and 51.

ACROSS

15. 52.

17 *rev.* 'And the Ruminant is preferable
surely to the Priest
Who battens on the woeful super-
stitions of the East,
The Mongol of the Monastery of
Shan.'

18. The name of one who made more
by standing on his head in Barce-
lona.

20. '. . . as a chattel: . . . in your daily
Account and economy; One with
your wines, And your books, and
your bath – . . . !' wrote Henley;
and look at the roads now!

26. Yews associated with ans.

27 *rev.* Thrill – baby girl?

30. The country in the preliminary note.

32. Look for the clue at the junction
of the Loire and the Cher.

34. My first is unchecked in 50 *dn.* and

my second in 45 *ac.*

35. The vulgar fellow has dropped an
article out of the equipage.

37. One kind of us the young who feel
us plant by strewing.

39 *rev.* There are old home and there
are old school.

40 *rev.* Lizard from Utah.

42 *rev.* Here's a halfpenny compensation
for turning your leg.

43. Where am I myself? At the
junction of the Loire and the Cher.

52. See 55.

54. See 3 and play with 10.

55. Beastly lucre with 52 *rev.*

56. Some consider the most desirable
part of the psalms.

58. On the 44 *rev.* side.

59. As a case in point, see 3.

62 *rev.* This trouble stands between
Kipling and the knife.

88

DOWN

2. My first is unchecked in 27, my second in 14 and my third in 42.

3. Belgian city before 54, makes a race for Albania before 59.

4 *rev.* This church becomes that kind of emporium in which speculators on a rise are not welcomed before 2.

6. See 63.

10. 'And every goose a swan, lad. And every . . . a queen.'

12, 13. Yes they, in Alsace? But they are not used in Greenland.

19. My first is unchecked in 36 and my second in 9.

23. We often feel this imported potted crane.

25 *rev.* Anna has a dozen of this dainty inside.

29. I'm thin and taller than 5's mother's sister.

33 *rev.* 23 on.

38. The girl who turned 10's head.

44 *rev.* This signature was appended twice to the Declaration of Independence.

45 *rev.* My last words are: 'Be wise and taste.'

48 *rev.* Vehicular substitute for soup.

49 *rev.* The agony of water in Hell.

57. Beast, say I sounding.

60, 54. The Sahiba called the Sahibs a strong-backed one.

61. 43.

63. Though I'm a bird with 6, I'm in the same place.

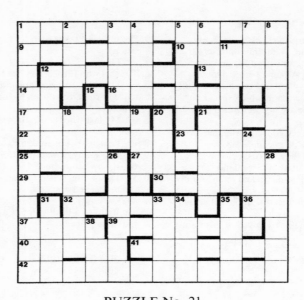

PUZZLE No. 21

'Birdless Grove' – one of Ximenes' last puzzles

ACROSS

1. *Wild bulbul doing reels is unkempt* (16).
9. Tay sure may be seen to emerge in one (7).
10. Ancient and modern activity shows rust (5).
12. (2 words) Mark, a disciple, agrees to serve (7).
13. Two old suppositions I ain't took in (4).
14. *Lizard: one summer month I'll come back* (6).
16. Cons U ops. like these? They're habitual (6).
17. *Always taking in X in a superficial way* (10).
21. *Scots know about insect producing jelly* (6).
22. *Choose a decorator for a low bus* (12).
23. Record that's precise about return of sloth (5).

25. *The cord, etc., is tangled – it's perverse* (10).
27. Fool's about crazy mad – it's the devil (7).
29. Prince has repulsed the bird girl (4).
30. *Trained digger has mixed piffle in basket* (10).
32. *Curiosity about bad round leads to mockery* (10).
36. *Caesar's ghost, entre les deux chambres?* (5).
37. Overcharge that's steep (4).
39. They're very hot – to cool is essential (7).
40. The heart of a big Scots town is in church (5).
41. *Frolic – no: I restrict: I'm a Scots head* (11).
42. *Alleged thief's for credit with wine people* (15).

90

1. *Colleges – Scots students cuddle princess up* (10).
2. Do is an old word for clamour (4).
3. *Bench with reputation that is flimsy* (8).
4. Seen in a deer-stalker – not nowadays (4)
*5. *Stupid person* (10).
6. This date is half obliterated (3).
7. Love boy being uppish, independent up north (4).
8. *Discordant tinny tone – he's no good* (9).
11. Block after being to press (7).
12. *One with depression at home, blue all round, on the rocks habitually* (10).
15. Its outcome may be cruel (5).
18. His partiality for a dance belied his name (7).
19. In U.S. he breaks in the old gee-gee (4).
20. *Buttress with poor stuff a low-cut garment* (7).
21. Nests – I had got in an unfinished one (5).
24. Robes discarded: do men go off such birds? (5).
25. *Eastern dress in unusual caps is spicy* (9).
26. No fun to be an M.P., we hear, in harmony (6).
28. *Odd cross between conger and wren is arched* (10).
31. Homer includes one – it's very tough (4).
33. *Please assume Carmichael was oracular* (8).
34. *Gape curiously about parrot – it's his bill* (8).
35. Monkey – there's a bird sitting on one (4).
38. *Nuclei that sound formidable in the army* (7).

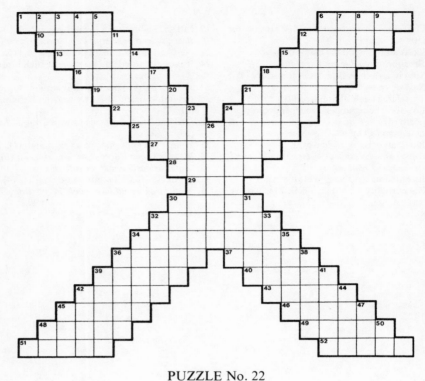

PUZZLE No. 22

In Memory of Ximenes

After the death of Ximenes (Derrick Macnutt), *The Observer* received many puzzles compiled by readers in his memory. This one was composed by a reader who calls himself Gong.

Every word is in *Chambers's Twentieth Century Dictionary*, Revised Edition, except one well-known proper name.

ACROSS

1. Young person – society prude (5).
6. Irish blasphemy, sire (5).
10. Ghastly old trumpet I had (5).
12. Cheerful of me to wander inside (5).
13. Ape one whose hand was freezing cold (5).
15. Plays some backing – it's involved, unlike Jagger and Co? (5)
16. Shift to scan in entrancement (5).
18. To walk backwards endlessly, scoring forty points (5).
19. Beer, and what it'll make you (5).
21. Three superfluous participants in twosome here? Required to warm bed (5).
22. Boom in counterfeit coins? (5)
24. Dense, and therefore requiring a hat (5).
25. Cinema in grip of violent spasm? They're acutely painful (9).
27. The groundsman often does his court, the tailor his coat (7).
28. Public protests (5).
29. Radar system giving initial indication of general enemy exercise (3).
30. Bachelor corporal perhaps has money in an account (5).
32. Spenser's guess perplexes English reader (7).
34. It gives edge to the news broadcast (9).
36. Mohammedan monarch going round his country's capital (5).
37. Easterly eastern ox (extinct) (5).
39. Platform ordered prior to delivery (5).
40. Musical fisherman with both ends forward secured (5).
42. Orally and aurally permissible (5).
43. Faithful about British backing tag (5).
45. Company involved in a soaking? Bail out (5).
46. It's 45 *dn.* without 'em – all back to front (5).
48. Advanced notice unit (5).
49. Mouldings around one Japanese gateway (5).
51. Cargo-ships usually are, long before port (5).
52. It's edible with goose or straw (5).

DOWN

2, 9, 48, 50 26 always did – but it had to be cracked (8).
3. Strange bottomless bottom (3).
4. If you need a device for exhibiting the spectrum, get her to cope (4).
5. Fishing-lines for scallops (5).
6. Make infatuated – that's what's nicest about love (5).
7. In father's time? (4).
8. Like a pub – one left out by brewer's cart (3).
9. See 2 *dn*.
11. Conferences aimed at improving the constitution? (5).
12. Powered velocipede proceeded aimlessly (5).
14. Noise made by emerging cork about to describe a parabola (5).
15. In Rome you prefer the throstle (5).
17. Paradoxical new epithet for Apollo (5).
18. Stems from copper railway now outdated (5).
20. Tried wrestling – all in (5).
21. Takes action about incipient sickness
23. Chortle widly about silver turning up in cabbage patch (9).
24. A pity, we hear – to E.E.C. sadly English is an unwelcome guest (9).
26. Exquisite tormentor for people after eleven on English sabbath? (7).
30. Livelihood, half of package deal for Roman populace (5).
31. Redolence from Italian flower, bottom uppermost (5).
32. One farm servant bringing up rear in Glasgow (5).
33. Record in charts? Rising single about top in rating (5).
34. Curlew what's almost seen rising (5).
35. If you've to make up a disinfectant, this'll be useful (5).
36. Treated to being included in rising parties (5).
38. Decay rising in evelenth month (5).
39. In need of 5p? Here's what Jock's unlikely to give, and what he'll give instead (5).
41. Discharge doctor in bed getting up (5).
42. Measure of land round about another (4).
44. Jock's learning a new reel (4).
45. Far from 12 *ac.*, exotic knives rise (3).
47. Gentleman in government without car (3).
48. See 2 *dn*.
50. See 2 *dn*.

93

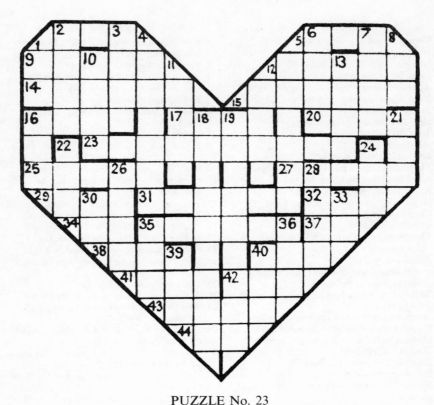

PUZZLE No. 23

'All Hearts' – a Listener *crossword by Gong*

Each clue contains a one-word definition or synonym of the answer to be entered in
the diagram but leads as a whole to another, longer word. For half the clues the
light is formed by removing the 'heart' (one or more letters) of the answer to the
whole clue and closing up the gap to form a new word. For the remaining clues the
'heart' alone (three or more letters) must be entered. In neither case do the discarded
letters necessarily form words. For the purposes of this puzzle the heart is exactly
central. Numbers in parentheses indicate the length of words to be entered in the
diagram. All words used directly or indirectly in the puzzle are in *Chambers's
Twentieth Century Dictionary Revised Edition* except two adverbial forms and, oddly,
the full answer to 15. Ignore accents.

ACROSS

1. Estimated surrounding raised railway with connections (5).
5. Bodices in so bustle's out – silly nit
has to leave (5).

9. Refuse backing in engagement?
Pop groups that do may (6).
11. Head of house? Gather that,
getting more experienced (6).

94

14. King nagged idly, sloping about in an undignified manner (7).
15. Obstructions may cause bells to go slack (no tolls, unfortunately) (7).
16. Impose extremes of variety on pasture-land, like trees (4).
17. A lum-hat's so adaptable as a receptacle (4).
20. Soak gripping cloth seen to shake – get him to pay the bill (4).
23. Such activity's healthy and super for us, catching foreign moke, love (10).
25. Observed returning ship; 'A very merry Christmas,' perhaps (5).
27. Spoil union with TV sera in the bloodstream (5).
29. Old surgical appliance twists triple ends of cotton ligatures (4).
31. Butchers' hooks for hocks of beasts (6).
32. Love stunt man in elaborate turn –

an old love story (4).
34. Little one's an addition to the brood – it's in disguise (3).
35. One must refrain from stewed Honduras cod's head and seaweed (6).
37. Russian community gets afraid, losing heart, before gazebo (3).
38. Wanting to take a leaf out of Reading's file? Could be (4).
40. I'll help in dyeing reversible dress as skirt for a doctor (4).
41. Beak, we hear, has to work at containing crime. Here's a minor one (4).
42. Type of ophthalmia exists – I flag almost, going back in (4).
43. What an idler does before the lady's holding in a shebeener (6).
44. Start to glide in drag and period trunks (4).

DOWN

1. Soggy English concoction without a sign of love for U.S. burglars (3).
2. Learning about English he's in trouble it isn't a refuge to weather (4).
3. Tardy poet possibly could be described as dragging this! (4)
4. What's fashioned in a criminal style (disputable)? I'll abstain (7).
5. Taxman's job: confusedly closet head of readers in two sorts of depression (7).
6. Essential participants in Boat Race, including member of XV? (4).
7. Nasty sore – tops of plant (ipecacuanha) good, applied internally, for that (4).
8. The means to curb or govern is in it (3).
10. Natural combination of sodium and titanium at hub of universe (4).
11. I was 'county' producing a lot of hollow moralising about principle of foxhunting (5).
12. Coarse silk that's rotten foils Parisienne (5).
13. Nile cutters? I had a bash with rigging about the yard (4).
16. All the wasting diseases are? Not necessarily true (4).

18. Ruinous hymnal covers start of offertory in a way that's not concordant (10).
19. Turned nasty, asking strangely, 'What businesses have corpses as subjects?' (10).
21. Gad, end of yawn is stifled by Malay two-master! (4).
22. Source of early British decoration is either side of mischievous goddess, detailed (4).
24. Pale-blue edible seaweed? That's about the utter limit (4).
26. Chaste garment is t-tempting, as before, showing ventilating partitions (5).
28. At edge of sleep disturb snorer. A gin fortifies (5).
30. 'Lack-lustre' isn't heard mistakenly (3).
33. Old reddish-brown pole, one in precious metal (poetic) (3).
35. Rich stuff about in pipeclay (4).
36. It'll serve to produce exotic strain (4).
39. Hypnotic power in a counterfeit utterance, reflected, may produce these (4).
40. One of high rank *dérangé*, crazy (4).

95

PUZZLE No. 24

'Cathedral Gossip and the Sound of Nudity' – a **Listener** *crossword by Sumydid*

Most of the completed diagram, it is clear, is inclined to justify the title, one way and another, limerically. Proper names, mostly familiar, are marked *, but 40 and 39–65 are in the Oxford Atlas. Two lights need apostrophes.

ACROSS

1.   The Listener's endowment is small according to us I recollected (8).

7.   The poet's *Illiad* (4).

10*. Northern isle named on 31, Piso Lisk principles (4).

11.   What the umpire said being left to sleep (4).

14.   So Scots lock up the piano divine! (4).

15.   A pike once got the rabble back (6).

16.   Hoe up hoe up at the bottom of the Bard's garden? (5).

18*. Isles that saw the reversal of the age a setback for the Carthaginians (7).

20.   Wine round about not not in the old ship in 'Cargoes' (3).

21–49. Bird's-eyes provide photo-electric cell with ten scallops (6).

21R–9. Point's point in points is pointed (4).

22.   Press close to blunder in the South-East (5).

96

25R. The ball was found so mounted copper got letter (4).

28. See 44R.

30R. Rod of authority opposed to nearly four rods (4).

31. Record to help farmers may be harrowing (4).

32. Describes day 'on the mountain tops' in *Romeo and Juliet* (4).

35. See 51 dn.

36–64*. Lady could accommodate English tenant providing tea for two (7).

37R–45. Journal's leader perversely heads stunt campaigns (6).

38. Bird joining parson, though his was the raven (3).

40*. Region of British Somaliland and what they said to the British! (3).

42–54. Point that had the gloomy Dean beat (6).

44R, 28. Show how V.I.P. collection varies (4, 3).

46. Obliged to dress back to front (3).

49. See 21.

51R. See 33R.

53. The sorrow that worries no hearts? (8).

57R–62. Idle Yard's poor produce (5).

58R. See 52.

59–56R. Rock-dwellers' anthem – 'Ours is a —— house, ours is' (6).

60. Painting struggles to follow Titian's opening (4).

63R–50. Grumble at rent being altered (6).

64. See 36 and 13.

65. See 39.

DOWN

1. The Listener is showing a range that's breezy (5).

2. Townsmen hiding Eastern names (5).

3*. In Oklahoma given a penny for treatment (5).

4*. Mixing drug at home for 'biggies' (6).

5–6. Sally so smart i.e. after swallowing small Scotch (6).

8R–61*. Part of Germany awaits help agitatedly (10).

9. See 21R.

12. Hail-storm in Orcadian bay (3).

13–64. Badge ornamental to candidate, possibly to steer (7).

14. If black-eyed she should (3).

17R. Decree to soften grain? On the contrary! (4).

19. A guy advised by Alpine village maiden (4).

23. See 41.

24. To earn for Milton see after 31 (3).

26R. See 50R.

27–43*. Relatively emergent in the nineties (8).

28R. In which Jonah was out of the fish's reach (4).

29–62. Keep a pound in the coal-scuttle (4).

33R–51R. Sprinkled oaths causing cough (5).

34. Triton's leader in the news (5).

38. Assume I stop moving (5).

39–65*. 18 nowadays could produce Italian flower (5).

41–23. To create vegetable extract TT stipulated stems (6).

41–48R. Screaming 'pieces of eight'? (7).

43. See 27.

45. See 37R.

47. 'O the floppin' droppin' ——' (Kipling) – awkward getting onto (4).

48R. See 41.

50. See 63R.

50R–26R*. He studied English and produced 'Hard Cash' (5).

51–35. Motor nerves heightened before any Tourist Trophy round the East (6).

52–58R. Take from wood spirits bivalent atoms (5).

54. See 42.

55. Porjects to stop English scrape (3).

56R. See 59.

61. See 8R.

62. See 29 and 57.

97

PUZZLE No. 25

'Full Board' by UtdtU – a Listener *crossword*

In each clue, the words preceding the comma form a normal definition of a four-letter word, the letters of which also appear, in a different order and not necessarily consecutively, in a later word. The lights are these four letters in the order in which they first appear in the later word, and are to be entered in turn on the square proper to the piece named and three consecutive moves appropriate to it. There is no castling and each pawn moves only in its own file. Each square is eventually used by two different pieces for the same letter.

WHITE

QRP	A Greek temple, at Monte Cassino?
QKtP	Scottish child, the gayest of lads.
QBP	A pretentious air, derisive.
QP	A great deal, at Yarmouth.
KP	Spenserian madman, relating his woes.
KBP	Thrust with foot, on tiptoe.
KKtP	Highland dagger, also found in Kingsbridge.
KRP	Dagger, carried by a whiskered Malayan.
QR	Heel over, not Bristol fashion.
QKt	Very small brook, no place for the Lorelei.
QB	Lower in estimation, to realists.
Q	Close with violence, upsetting the calmest nerves.
K	Pet lamb, cared for by the farmer's wife.
KB	Serenity of feelings, without complaint.
KKt	Mischievous sprite, unpacking Pandora's box.
KR	Magnifying glass, used by Landseer.

BLACK

QRP   To intrude as an uninvited guest, in the laird's stronghold.

QKtP   A Spenserian light, not lately used.

QBP   Bind to secrecy, in client's interest.

QP   A bagpipe composition, from my repertoire.

KP   To swallow greedily, an ungentlemanly habit.

KBP   The fashion, for mademoiselle.

KKtP   Travel on a broomstick, with eldrich shrieks.

KRP   To practise crystal-gazing, as in Yorkshire.

QR   Rapid drumbeat, but rallentando.

QKt   The militia of Old England, a friendly lot.

QB   Queer person, unrecognised.

Q   Formerly ale with wormwood, a perilous mixture.

K   Strain at the bit, not very helpful.

KB   Pillar of coal left in mine, as a support.

KKt   Worry over trifles, successfully.

KR   An immature eel, unsightly.

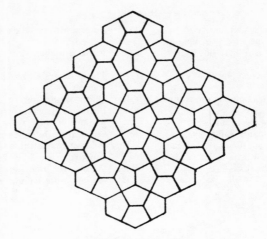

PUZZLE No. 26

'Hexa-Pentagonal' – a puzzle by Croton from The Listener

The diagram of 64 pentagons will be found to resolve itself into 16 horizontal hexagons, intersected by 9 complete vertical hexagons with portions of others.

In a letter is placed inside each pentagon, every hexagon forms a word of four letters when read clockwise. Further, the 8 pentagons along each of the four boundaries, *i.e.* those included in horizontal hexagons only, give an eight-letter word when read from corner to corner in a clockwise direction.

The horizontal hexagons are clued in order starting from the top, proceeding from left to right in successive rows. Similarly, the vertical hexagons start on the left and proceed from top to bottom in successive columns.

HORIZONTAL HEXAGONS

1. Rouse.
2. Healthy.
3. Priest
4. Grain.
5. Cargo.
6. Fruit.
7. Where Rachel wept.
8. Unsatisfactory.
9. Old war weapon.
10. Small valley.
11. Stern.
12. Plant.
13. Jack.
14. . . . majesty.
15. Fine filaments.
16. Set of three.

VERTICAL HEXAGONS

1. Arab governor.
2. Container.
3. Ruins.
4. Sediment.
5. Innocent person.
6. Part of Erin.
7. Winglike.
8. Redclyffe had one.
9. Chalk.

BOUNDARY WORDS
(8 letters)

1. Panic flight.
2. More than Super Royal.
3. Message.
4. Seamen.

100

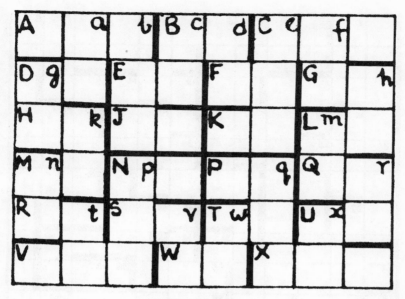

PUZZLE No. 27

'Equations' by Trand – from The Listener

The lights are positive integral solutions of the following equations.
In symmetrical expressions, the roots are in ascending order of magnitude.
Capital letters refer to clues across, and small letters to clues down. There is no
factor common to all the numbers in each set.

1. $(H/J)^3 + Q^3 = x^3 + m^3$.
2. $f^3 + d^3 = G^3 + v^3$.
3. $t^3 + (T+1)^3 = c^3 + (F-1)^3$.
4. $R^3 = S^3 + k^3 + B3$.
5. $J^3 = K^3 + S^3 + D^3$.
6. $(2t)^3 = W^3 + L^3 + N^3$.
7. $h^3 = (G-1)^3 + G^3 + B^3$.
8. $(G-1)^3 = x^3 + r^3 + (2g-1)^3$.
9. $A^3 = 1 + V^3 + (2B)^3$.
10. $G^4 + e^4 = q^4 + C^4$.
11. $X^4 = L^4 + (4L)^4 + b^4 + p^4$.
12. $n^2 + (5P)^2 = a^2 + 2U^2$.
$\qquad\qquad = t^2 + 3M^2$.
$\qquad\qquad = E^2$.
13. $(c+2)^2 + (a+1)^2 = (n-1)^2 + 2k^2$.
$\qquad\qquad\qquad = 1 + 3H^2$.
$\qquad\qquad\qquad = w^2$.

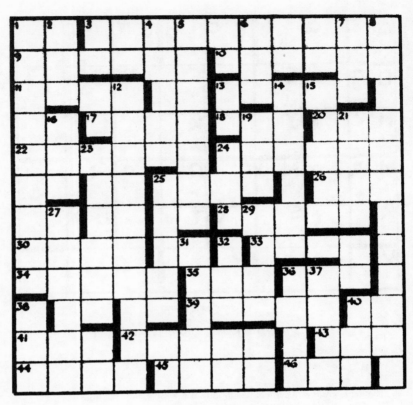

PUZZLE No. 28

'Word Sums' – *a puzzle from* The Listener *by Proton*

Note: In each of the sums below, each letter represents a different digit. The same letter indicates the same digit throughout a sum, but not throughout the puzzle. These digits are to be entered in the diagram.

A.   3A   38D   5D
$$\text{FRUITDEMON} \div \text{FOE} = \text{INTROIT}$$

B.   9A   40D   43A
$$\text{NIBBLE} = \text{CAT} + \text{BAG}$$

C.   10A   4D   15D
$$\text{FLORIN} = \text{PENCE} + \text{CROWN}$$

D.   11A   36A 46A
$$\text{ABCD} = \text{EFG} + \text{HIJ}$$

E.   13A   16D   18A   12D
$$\text{ASWIM} \times \text{AWN} \times \text{MNA} = \text{ASARABACCA} - (C \times R^N \times A^R \times N^O)$$

F.   17A = 30A 36D 33A
$$\text{LOST} = \text{BALL} + \text{OVER}$$

G.   20A 26A 35A 29D   25A 41A
$$\text{USE} + \text{EKE} + \text{PAS} + \text{POST} = \text{PETS} + \text{TUT}$$

H.   22A   23D
$$\text{NECTAR} + \text{CHORAL} = \text{TRANCE}$$

I.   24A   34A
$$\text{VERMIN} = \text{FLIER} + \text{LANCE}$$

J.   28A   31D   32D
$$\text{SEEPS} - \text{SESIA} = \text{SPY}$$

K.   39A   42A   45A   1D
$$(\text{TOILS} + \text{STIRS}) \times \text{PERI} = \text{ASTROPHEL}$$

L.   44A   37D   24D
$$\text{AMOS} = \text{ADAM} + \text{EVE}$$

M.   2D 19D 21D
$$\text{TOE} + \text{ROD} = \text{DEED}$$

N.   6D   7D   27D
$$\text{TIE} \times \text{NEW} = \text{TERETE}$$

O.   8D   14D   25D
$$\text{RESINIFEROUS} - 4000 = (\text{SIFFLE} + \text{LUFFS})^2$$

A M	N	O	P	Q	R	S	T	U	V	W	X
B											
C											
D											
E											
F											
G											
H											
I											
J											
K											
L											

PUZZLE No. 29

'Overlapping' – another tough one from The Listener

The lights in each line of the diagram overlap (e.g. in the line Z, which when completed might read ORANGELIDESK, clue Z1 would lead to light ORANGE, Z2 to GELID, Z3 to ELIDE, and Z4 to DESK.)

A1. A beast of the Nepal if not yet is.
  2. English Egyptian is in U.S. this.

B1. The vendor's room the caller's heart makes vext.
  2. Girl O for clue a trial 'tis if next'd.
  3. Form blunt round shape, see J2 if perplex'd.

C1. Cry mortal's death bade by a king who'd wined.
  2. Pearl's parent has the dictionary defined.
  3. Rule of dark Latin river here we find.

D1. The bonds make Cromwell dateless seen.
  2. A critic, well, Knight's widow'd been.
  3. Desire ten dollar's bird I mean.
  4. It came Crawley and Sharp between.

E1. Plays skilfully, less skilfully their charge.
  2. A self-confessed dark Latin island large.

F1. Seems I know E1 of god.
  2. Aquatic mammals tetrapod.
  3. Was Scotsman charged too much for rod?

G1. Old god to whom 'twas not design.
  2. Dry metamorphosed god opine.
  3. The eggs of metal bearing tine.
  4. B3 a stream of which we dine.
  5. Sign five with nine for such a line.

H1. Harsh one small poet B3s to two therefor.
  2. End of C1 is inches twenty-four?
  3. Twopence assessed, three quarters coin of yore.

I1. Balder his wife, a girl at heart and head.
  2. In this if empty; oversea L3 instead.
  3. Before if bus is ta'en home of the dead.
  4. A crown of gold or silver, accent's shed.
  5. Almost a clue; let clue for clue be read.

J1. A poker clergyman, Q T1 mess.
  2. To B3, or the end of U1 guess.
  3. Smear fish that has turned bad to meet success.
  4. Is next, but inasmuch disjoined much less.

K1. In inner thrice, near thrice endmost is found.
  2. Vessel that with tar weighs a hundred pound.
  3. Opposed to dozens, less than dozen round.

L1. About the foreign door send down again.
  2. Series of years are B3ed I thus maintain.
  3. Take moles from kind of treacle; beast obtain.

M1. Contracted searching clue of ice in hand.
  2. Praising his art 'the people sit and stand'.

N1. 'Pleasant to know' a comic rhymer prime.
  2. Three times were kept in such a rhyme.
  3. Three times Othello cried motive of crime.

O1. Saint's light on mast; beyond the tree nought had.
  2. There's nought in M1's steed to make him sad.
  3. Inscribe upon the list, the name just add.

P1. These may be drawn, hatch'd, issued quarterly.
  2. Unrelenting and to wor may be.
  3. Apparently B3 8 into 3.

Q1. Three miles ? abroad seven hundred years ago.
  2. Put end to a contention old will do.
  3. H was; the end of next will surely show.
  4. It bears first fleece, fore men a covering too.

R1. The isles of Hindustani chief.
  2. Stupid solution sounds in brief.
  3. = L2.

S1. Done with great T4 form on map is read.
  2. Half century here preferred to haycat said.
  3. Put out the ebb, transposed wherewith we're fed.

T1. Allowance changed allowance still gives me.
  2. Measures a river great of Germany.
  3. Over this prophet boss or riddles see.
  4. Would 70 yds. approx. the answer be?

U1. Repeated sum of T1 and S3.
  2. Exclude from livelihood we eat can be.

V1. A fifth, a pound a hundredweight for you.
  2. One hundred thousand over one; no clue.

W1. Drive rising 'ere No Trump with fool to lead.
  2. = D3.
  3. Another bird to strive with late you'll need.
  4. They're k and p and t refuse to plead.

X1. A shape uncommon here you'll view.
  2. Birds' Unfledged homes and downies' too.

9. Crosswords With a Message

Seven days before D-Day in 1944, an M.I.5 officer sat down to tackle the *Daily Telegraph* crossword. Not that he was doing it for relaxation. Seldom, if ever, has a crossword been attended to with greater concentration, for studying the clues had suddenly become one of the officer's most important duties. In the tense days before the invasion of Europe, the *Daily Telegraph*'s cryptic clues were giving the war planners a bad case of jitters.

During the month of May, the UTAH and OMAHA had appeared as solutions. Both names were secret code words chosen for Normandy landing beaches. Then on Saturday, May 27th, the clue '—but some bigwig like this has stolen some of it at times' yielded the answer OVERLORD . . . the code name for the whole D-Day operation! What would this morning's clues throw up? How about 11 Across: 'This bush is a centre of nursery revolutions'? Sure enough, MULBERRY . . . the code name for the two giant harbours that were to be towed across the Channel.

M.I.5.'s nerves were jangled further in a couple of days when 15 Across ('Britannia and he hold to the same thing') produced the code name for D-Day's naval operations: NEPTUNE.

Two M.I.5 men set out for the Surrey home of Leonard Sidney Dawe, who for twenty years had been the chief crossword compiler for the paper. How could he explain the use of five highly confidential code names within one month, all of them relating to the D-Day invasion? Fortunately, Dawe was able to convince them that it was all a fantastic coincidence!

Coincidence reared its puzzling head more recently when the

Barbara Windsor makes an attractive setting for the
Sunday Times *Crossword.*

name of the road outside Wormwood Scrubs Prison – Artillery
Row – appeared in *The Times* crossword, just two days before
master spy George Blake escaped over the wall. Once again,
M.I.5 investigated the possibility that the nation's early morning
recreation might be being exploited by the nation's enemies. In

Hungary in 1925 all newspaper crosswords had to be submitted for official scrutiny as a precaution against Royalist subversion. During the Second World War, the War Office is reported to have banned the appearance of crosswords from newspapers going to the Dominions, for security reasons. A month after the liberation of Paris, crosswords were forbidden from the Paris newspapers in case they might be used for fifth column messages. While these fears might seem preposterous, the fact is that crosswords were used by underground anti-Nazi propagandists in Germany in 1934, as a secret method of communicating with each other.

In 1930 a reader of *The Times* about to take a motoring trip on the Continent tore the crosswords from the paper to give himself something to do in the evenings. On crossing the Italian frontier he was met by a Fascist officer who presumably hadn't seen crosswords before. The officer, finding one puzzle half completed, angrily accused the Englishman of being a spy, confiscated the puzzles and refused to stamp his passport.

From time to time, governments have made use of the crossword as a tool of propaganda, the first such puzzles having appeared in Soviet Russia in January, 1934. The message in such puzzles tends to be rather heavy handed. An example from the Soviet magazine *Ogonyok* dating from the height of the Cold War in the 1950's gives the following clues:

'What warmongers fear more than anything else.'
    Solution: 'Peace'.
'The American puppet in the Bonn circus.'
    Solution: 'Adenauer'.
'A bird persecuted for un-American activity.'
    Solution: 'Dove'.
'The street in which warmongers dwell.'
    Solution: 'Wall'.

In the little booklets of crossword puzzles that were selling at the same time in East Germany for one penny, the clues were no more inspired:

'Who rescued the Chinese labourers from slave labour?'
    Solution: 'Mao'.

One newspaper crossword that must have given its East

PUZZLE No. 30

The V-1 Puzzle

ACROSS

1. He is your enemy, too.
7. V-1 is so fast, that it is hard to this.
8. Partly a beverage.
10. This is the beginning of a German victory.
11. We hear that this is a rare commodity in England.
13. This is in Latin.
14. He wants all you've got.

DOWN

1. In the case of the air war, he has been bit by V-1.
2. Money, but no pence.
3. Men and material intended for Normandy very often finish up at the bottom of this.
4. V-1 contains this.
5. Britain has none at inter-Allied conferences.
6. At Teheran, Churchill practically did this before Stalin.
9. First person singular.
10. Two reprisals with nothing in between.
12. Warmongers must this, if England is to be saved.
13. That man.

German readers some amusement was the one that gave the solution 'Tito' to the clue 'A European statesman'. A few days later the paper printed a complete column of apology and self-criticism, shamefacedly admitting that the crossword had been supplied by a non-Communist syndicate in Berlin. 'You can see how cleverly the imperialist propagandists squeeze anti-communist propaganda even into such non-political things as crosswords.'

The renowned German lack of humour was even more evident in such clues as 'He wants all you've got' (Solution: 'Roosevelt') printed on crosswords that were delivered free of charge to puzzle enthusiasts in the South of England in January, 1945. These puzzles were scattered from a V1 buzz-bomb, the black squares of the crossword grid being designed to form the letters V1. Perhaps the Nazis got the idea from the letter written to *The Times* by Sir Reginald Mart in 1936. Sir Reginald drew attention to the opportunity given by the crossword for propaganda purposes and pointed out that in the crossword of January 8, the centre-piece of the design was a clearly marked swastika. This symbol reared its ugly head again in 1970 when it was featured at the centre of the silver trophy given to the prizewinner of the *Cutty Sark/Times* Crossword Championship.

Governments occasionally use crosswords for more acceptable forms of propaganda – crosswords to sell the message of fire prevention have been employed in the United States – but it is the commercial propagandists, the advertising agencies, who are most successful in using the crossword to get a message across. The following crossword advertisement was one of a series produced by the Leicester agency, Frank Gayton Advertising Limited, to promote their client, a well-known building society. The advertisements appeared only in journals aimed at solicitors, accountants, bank managers and investors, and as these readers are fully aware of the advantages of saving with a building society, the agency was able to concentrate on putting across their client's name in an unusual and fairly light hearted way.

Readers of *The Times* were startled on June 5th, 1972, to find what appeared to be the paper's page of classified advertisements with its normal column headings – but without any classified advertisements! The only thing that appeared to be in place was the crossword in the bottom left corner. Even the crossword turned out to be not what it seemed. The clues and their solutions spelled out amusing messages on the value of butter, and in fact the entire page, including the crossword, was an eye-catching advertisements for butter.

When you're toiling with *The Times* crossword, you soon run out of space writing trial answers in the narrow margins of the page. That's why it is particularly helpful when you find a blank space thoughtfully provided in a charity advertisement alongside

3 down holds the clue to the perfect investment for your customers. Something offering complete security and a good rate of tax-paid interest, plus ready availability of their capital.

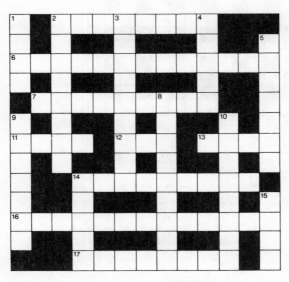

ACROSS

2. See 3 down.
6. Highlights of the western. (8, 5)
7. That's why! (3, 6)
11. Monstrous person. (4)
12. Look in torment for a rocky peak. (3)
13. The Frenchman's lady friend. (4)
14. See 3 down.
16. Muddled post traps mink in silence. (8, 5)
17. Late dice can be fragile. (8)

DOWN

1. Put a question on attitude. (4)
2. Sons of my father. (8)
3. 14 across, 2 across, 9. Confused girl entices city men to bare up in Leeds. (9, 9, 8, 7)
4. Mount and progress. (3, 2)
5. Land in the States. (7)
8. Wounding verbal scar I cast. (9)
9. See 3 down.
10. Cardinal address. (8)
14. Scottish musak? (5)
15. The nature goddess is repeated. (4)

PUZZLE No. 31

A crossword advertisement giving the answer to investment problems

111

The Times Crossword Puzzle No 13,047

A Surgeon's Skill

ACROSS

1 Criminal activity in which a prince engaged (9).

6 Like filling one container from another (5).

9 Odour of sanctity—how it might anger one (7).

10 Does without money or a girl (7).

Help to remove piano and change accommodation

crane shifted

a politi-

on

4 Ruth—a sea nymph in disguise (8).

5 Youth in German capital billed as cargo (6).

6 Dance wear ? (6).

7 Killer is a foreigner, about fifty (9).

8 Sounds a dandy poet ! (5).

14 Where I chuck my weight about in London (9)

16 Girl's service book in the boot (9).

17 Report a killer in the end (8).

18 Knew old song of the climber ? (8).

21 Many cut as meat might be (6).

is backward—no

ts ? (5).

An aid to solvers: a blank space in the adjacent advertisement

the puzzle—as in the example shown opposite for an advertisement inserted by the Royal College of Surgeons of England. Inevitably, of course, your eye is drawn to the important message from the Appeal Secretary of the charity.

When Max Raynor combined five companies to form Combined Graphic Services Limited, he mailed a series of giant calendars month by month to existing and prospective clients to promote the new company name. The puzzle overleaf, measuring a handsome 23″ × 15″, was designed by Stuart Hasted to include the initials CGS in the pattern of squares. Max Raynor doesn't know if anyone completed the crossword although he had many clients ringing up demanding the solutions of particular clues. Two television producers phoned to point out an unfortunate spelling error in the answer to 26 Across. (It should be 'i' in the third letter, but the compiler made it an 'e'.)

ACROSS

2 Happy? No. (3)
5 U.S. State. (5)
9 Did they see red? (5)
13 One of our many assets. (1.3)
14 Standby defence, at cost. (3.1.1)
15 Not 'way out'. (5)
16 This bird can't fly and is not well endowed. (3)
17 That little devil's back. (3)
18 It makes reason. (5)
22 Is this a speedy opera? (5)
26 An American 'commercial' award. (4)
27 These don't jam up our studio. (5.3)

28 A measure of hot air. (5)
29 Initially is this a slum flat? (1.1.3)
30 Two fruits seen in reverse. (4)
31 You will need to get this answer write. (3)
32 German drink. (4)
33 Our version of it is Allegretto. (5)
34 Hang it. (5)
35 They say it leads to good health. (3)

37 We always aim for this award. (1.2)
39 The measures of some of our work. (3)
40 Is this a proof— and unkind to Andy? (1.1)
42 The reverse of down.(2)
43 A shortened scale of art. (3)
44 The precise measure of 43 across. (5.2)
45 Fred, Bert or Basil's other half. (5)
46 A short reference to her Majesty. (1.1.1)
47 Do this to us. (3)

DOWN

1 The Combined Graphics way of avoiding disappointing 'strip shows'. (5.10)
3 Rush jobs call for these letters. (1.1.1)
4 The reverse of our artists' reputation. (9.6)
5 They keep us abreast of events on one side of the channel. (1.1.1)
6 Our labs life blood. (3)
7 Applicable. (3)

8 Does this cause a 'Yanky' car to stall. (1.3)
9 Those others. (4)
10 Is this for real? (3)
11 A King artist either way. (1.2)
12 Straightforward, no? (3)
19 Scared? Not exactly the hue. (5)
20 Do we look for this in a 'birds' eye. (5)
21 Our contact, for example. (1.1.3)
23 A sound visual. (5)
24 Penthouse storey. (5)
25 Initially, artists prefer not to work this way. (1.1.3)
27 37 across is part of this. (3)

36 This is not insignificant in the game. (4)
38 Will the beast feel this too pointed. (4)
41 We aim to serve these every time. (4)

The simple solution to every kind of artwork from dye transfers to key lines is found under Combined Graphic Services Limited.

PUZZLE No. 32

A crossword calendar issued by C.G.S., a design group

10. Variants of the Crossword

One Friday in 1934 a lady walked into the Madison Avenue offices of *The Saturday Review of Literature* with a bundle of papers under her arm. 'I've invented a new type of crossword puzzle,' Elizabeth Kingsley explained. 'I thought you might like to try them in the magazine. I call them Double Crostics.' An associate editor took them home for the weekend, cogitated a couple of days and decided to give it a whirl. The puzzle was an instant success – one of the few American puzzles that demand of their readers more than to solve simple definitions. Over the next eighteen years Elizabeth Kingsley contributed 975 Double Crostics to *The Saturday Review*, never missing a single issue. During that time, she also compiled twenty-six books of Double Crostics, requiring some 2,500 puzzles. On November 29th 1952, she retired, handing her post on the magazine to her successor, Doris Nash Wortman. In May 1953, while the papers on both sides of the Atlantic were full of the preparations for the forthcoming coronation of Queen Elizabeth II, the Editors of the *Saturday Review* decided to publish a tribute to Mrs. Kingsley as 'our own Queen Elizabeth'. The tribute, which coincided with the publication of Double Crostic Number 1,000, appeared none too soon; Mrs. Kingsley died a few days after its publication.

A puzzle very similar in concept to the Double Crostic – the Leadergram – ran for many years in Britain, first in *The Leader*, a competition paper, then in the much-missed *Picture Post*. Leadergrams appear monthly nowadays in *Ideal Home* and are compiled by David Bates who inherited the task from his father.

One English variant of the crossword is, sadly, no longer with

115

PUZZLE No. 33

The Saturday Review's *first Double-Crostic*

DIRECTIONS – To solve this puzzle, you must guess twenty-five words, the definitions of which are given in the column headed DEFINITIONS. The letters in each word to be guessed are numbered (these numbers appear at the beginning of each definition) and you are thereby able to tell how many letters are in the required word. When you have guessed a word each letter is to be written in the correspondingly numbered square on the puzzle diagram. When the squares are all filled in you will find (by reading from left to right) a quotation from a famous author. Reading up and down, the letters mean nothing! The black squares indicate ends of words; therefore words do not necessarily end at the right side of the diagram.

Either before (preferably) or after placing the letters in their squares you should write the words you have guessed on the blank lines which appear to the right in the column headed WORDS. The initial letters of this list of words spell the name of the author and the title of the piece from which the quotation has been taken.

116

DEFINITIONS		WORDS

DEFINITIONS

I.   1-14-23-50-95. A perfume of roses.

II.   145-6-28-90-137. Child's game played with cards and numbers.

III.   97-8-79-146-98-61-75-77-76-32-27-19-133. Light as a feather.

IV.   80-85-60-113-51-58-48. Held in high esteem; worshipped.

V.   81-172-31-84-24-176-65-89. Insubstantial.

VI.   112-45-114-164-149-173-142-36. The business section of a city.

VII.   144-102-2-63. Material for bandages.

VIII.   37-4-66-82-110-116-62. Upholstered backless seat.

IX.   100-106-33-5-122-41-138-69-83-13-162-127. A Russian pianist.

X.   40-59-52-25. A drupe with a single seed.

XI.   135-175-3-73. Movement of the ocean.

XII.   130-43-129-107-111-55-139-47. To alienate.

XIII.   15-121-92-136-101-39. A mighty hunter.

XIV.   167-9-140-46-105. Artless; simple.

XV.   119-54-104-17-153-34. Hebrew God.

XVI.   134-63-128-168-16-30. Flat, dark image.

XVII.   155-125-78-148-143-165-158-56. Prejudiced (compound).

XVIII.   12-96-120-11-7-170-150-21-68-174. Significant, unusual.

XIX.   87-141-171-161-67-20-10-126. Not propitious.

XX.   177-99-152,163-108-115. Member of the tribe of Levi.

XXI.   42-88-26-159-49-91. Doodle dandy.

XXII.   22-71-151-118-131-147-38-94-160-29. Watchword (Bibl.).

XXIII.   109-86-132-124-72-117-123-178. Uttered a harsh sound.

XXIV.   157-44-93-53-166-18-35-103. Forceful.

XXV.   156-154-74-169-70-57. To stop the flow.

WORDS

I. _____

II. _____

III. _____

IV. _____

V. _____

VI. _____

VII. _____

VIII. _____

IX. _____

X. _____

XI. _____

XII. _____

XIII. _____

XIV. _____

XV. _____

XVI. _____

XVII. _____

XVIII. _____

XIX. _____

XX. _____

XXI. _____

XXII. _____

XXIII. _____

XXIV. _____

XXV. _____

A Let apeman order a sign-board. — 98 14 120 136 52 82 5 110 67

B Last with a point under confusion. — 3 36 109 74 137 16

C Heavy stuff to show the way. — 122 86 18 6

D Insubstantial—but perceived on conversion. — 8 28 63 116 130

E Nothing between vessel and den? Not true! — 17 61 115 2 88 29 100 76 45

F Poultry she turned into stuffing. — 32 121 44 97 69 84 22 108 54 11

G Assents sleepily. — 26 38 78 i

H It's more than just a pad. Observe the volume! — 90 131 58 72 19 41 111 27

I Cotton stripped is worn here, it seems. — 75 4 68 106 46 91 132 56 15 117

J A descendant loses it, naturally. — 24 128 92 34 60 104

K HUNTS A SITE (anag) — 125 33 59 112 89 12 70 103 47 134

L Just a moment, it's urgent. — 25 65 127 39 48 94 55

M The kit for someone going flat out? — 57 119 30 135 105 43 95 9 81

N A trunk—or top part of trunk. — 13 66 80 118 23

O Clumsy as Venus de Milo! — 21 62 31 10 49 129 83

P Unoccupied space chamber. — 101 35 133 51

Q "How his —— stands, who knows save heaven?" (Hamlet) — 126 42 79 64 93

R Where to clean a torn hat in a sweeper. — 73 7 37 85 114 20 53 102

S Those left in it may get quite a jolt. — 96 77 107 124 40

T The likeness often gives a capital impression. — 113 87 71 50 99 123

PUZZLE No. 34

A recent 'Leadergram' from Ideal Home

Write the answers to the clues in the panel next to them (not in the puzzle itself). Then write the individual letters of each word, according to their numbers, in the puzzle itself. Reading downwards the initial letters of the words in the completed panel make up the name of an author and the title of one of his (or her) works. And the completed puzzle design – left to right – gives a quotation from the same work, the words being separated by black squares.

us. This was the Double Acrostic, invented by Hubert Phillips and inspired by the nineteenth-century word square puzzle of the same name. The Phillips Double Acrostic had, according to its inventor's claim, the same relationship to the traditional crossword as the relationship of whist to bridge. Whist, he contended, is a more elegant and more difficult game than bridge; at the same time its mechanics are less elaborate. Similarly an acrostic is more elegant and normally more difficult to solve than a crossword, yet its presentation is ostensibly simpler. In *Word Play*, a 1945 Penguin collection of puzzles compiled by Hubert Phillips, a typical Double Acrostic is:

UPRIGHTS

Here's my Lord; here, Sir, are you.
Of Each, to start with, give me two.

LIGHTS

1. He wears his 'lorals' on the Bench.
2. A 'British King' begat the wench.
3. A tasty melange now display.
4. The novelist has lost his way.
5. One chapter's all that I can show.
6. One script on top and one below.

In a Double Acrostic, Phillips always gave his clues in verse. But more important, no crossword diagram was offered to the reader. Phillips points out, however, that puzzlers would be quite at home with the same puzzle if it were presented in a slightly different form:

1. He wears his 'lorals' on the Bench (4).
2. A 'British King' begat the wench (6).
  and so on . . .

DOWN
1 & 7. Here's My Lord; here, Sir, are you.
  Of each, to start with, give me two (6, 6).

This is still an odd crossword, of course. There are only two
clues 'down'. And the clues 'across' are only related to the 'down'
clues in terms of their first and last letters. Thus the Double
Acrostic has two distinguishing features: first, there are only two
vertical clues – the 'Uprights' – and we can deduce how many
letters there are in each by the number of 'Lights'; secondly, each
'Light' may have any number of letters. In the solution to the
example above, they range from four to ten.

```
B   E   A       K
I   M O G E     N
S A L M A G U N D I
H   E   M   I N G WAY
O   B   A   D I A H
P   A L I   M P S E S T
```

Note that Light 4, yields the solution: Heming(way). It is permissible to play tricks like this with the Lights – beheading or
curtailing the words – as long as an appropriate hint is given in
the clue. Double Acrostics were popular during the Second
World War, when they appeared in two papers *The Puzzler* and
The Sphinx at Play. Both papers are long since defunct (another
magazine entitled *The Puzzler* has recently appeared, but has no
connection with its predecessor). Since Phillips' death the Double
Acrostic has not been taken up by other puzzle compilers which
is somewhat surprising in view of its attractiveness both to
puzzlers and to puzzle editors who are freed from the constraint
of having to print a crossword grid. The explanation can
probably be found when one realises that puzzle compilers of
Hubert Phillips' ability are few and far between.

Phillips was born in 1891 and won distinction in History and

Economics at Oxford. From 1919 to 1924 he was Head of the Department of Economics at Bristol University and Director of Extra-Mural Studies. He then went into politics and became Secretary and Adviser to the Liberal Parliamentary Party. He entered Fleet Street at the mature age of 38, becoming known to a wide public as Dogberry of the *News Chronicle* and Caliban of the *New Statesman*. Phillips also contributed a wide variety of word puzzles, mathematical puzzles and logic puzzles to the *Star*, the *Daily Telegraph*, the *Evening Standard*, *Truth* and even the *Law Journal*.

PUZZLE No. 35

A double acrostic

UPRIGHTS

This kept – well, schoolboys oft declaim
    His feat, in stanzas pat;
But what he kept is not the same
    As is the same as that.

LIGHTS

1. This cheerily suggests the horse.
2.   A bishop's to and fro.
3. So near wrapped up, yet great in force.
4.   Sum up? or – in you go!
5. I part, you see, from this strange beast.
6.   Go, go(awretch sublime).
7. In such discover this at least.
8.   The climax of the climb.

121

PUZZLE No. 36

A Double Acrostic

UPRIGHTS

Will you put an appearance in?
(About the time they do begin!)

LIGHTS

1. Mercury's that:
   So is a bat.
2. R.L.S.
   You may guess.
3. The creature exists, I'm assured,
   Though it certainly sounds like a fraud.
4. What *should* be learnt in a letter?
   In this case a firearm had better!
5. That of the Dong
   Gave a light (in the song).

An interesting variant of the word square is the Jaxsquare, invented in the late 1930's by John Matthews and published by a Liverpool newsagent. This owed its origin to a combination of sources. The first of these is a game called 'Poker Crosswords' for two players. In this game, each player having pencil and paper draws four straight lines crossing four other straight lines so as to make twenty-five empty squares. A coin is tossed and the player winning the toss has the right to choose the first of twenty-five letters to be inserted into the squares. They go on alternately naming letters so as to make words of five letters (worth 10 points), four letters (5 points) and three letters (2 points). Eighty points is considered a very good score, especially if your opponent offers a J, an X or a Q half way through the game.

Developed from this, a Liverpool newspaper ran a competition for a short time, entitled 'Twenty-fives'. Readers were given twenty-five letters, usually in the form of a well-known saying like 'Rolling stones gather no moss', and invited to send in completed word squares using these letters. No competitor was successful in fully completing a square to score 100 points. Intrigued by this, Matthews wondered if it was at all possible to

122

provide a sensible phrase from which a 100-point score could be generated and realised that the way to start was to construct a complete word square first and then re-arrange the letters to form a phrase. Matthews' first Jaxsquare and the accompanying phrase are shown below:

S T E M S
C O V E T
A W A R E   'TO C.S.M. TAP-WATER
R E D I P   IS SERVED FREE'.
F R E T S

In 1960 he collected together enough phrases to construct a hundred Jaxsquares and put them in a little book sold from the newsagent's shop. In *The Story of the Jaxsquare* to make things easy for the reader, Matthews at the beginning of the book constructs part of the square for you – in effect, giving you a help of 76%. As the book progresses, the percentage of the puzzles already completed grows steadily smaller until eventually you are given just the twenty-five letter phrase and you have to build the complete word-square yourself.

PUZZLE No. 37

Complete the Jaxsquare

S T R I P
C R A N E
R A N G   'CAR RE-ENTERS RACING
A C T   PAST POST'
P E

PUZZLE No. 38

Build Jaxsquares from the following phrases

'NOTED PORKERS AMAZE HERCULES'

'SERVE TABLE ALL SUMMER IN CLUB'

The earliest variant on the conventional crossword was the bilingual crossword with English clues and answers in French. Examples can be found in books published within a few months of the emergence of the crossword craze. Later examples include Biblical crosswords in religious papers and English/Yiddish crosswords in New York papers. Canadian newspapers often print crosswords in which the horizontal words have French clues and English answers, while the vertical words have English clues and French answers. Perhaps the most intriguing is a book of educational crosswords in which the clues are in English and the answers in Japanese pictography, although a strong rival might be the puzzle which employed a mixture of words and symbols:

♡ ache   ◇ Lil   ♡ beat   ♠ work   ♣ man   ♠ bid

The *Daily Telegraph* crossword compiler, D. St. P. Barnard, in his book *Anatomy of the Crossword* describes a remarkable puzzle created by Norman Gray of Cheam, Surrey. This puzzle, which took two years to compile, is a 15 × 15 × 15 crossword made of 3,375 'squares' containing hundreds of words clued across, down and through!

A simpler three-dimensional word-game was sold by Partridge's Models Limited in the early 1930's. This consisted of twenty-seven blocks each with a letter on five sides, and a number on the sixth side. The numbers have no bearing on the solution and are for identification purposes only. The blocks are arranged so that they stand numbered side down. They are then divided into three groups of nine. Each group of nine must be arranged in a magic square to form three letter words horizontally, vertically and round the four sides – ten words on each group.

The next step is to place the three layers one above the other without altering the position of the letters, to form a magic cube. The five exposed faces will now read with three-letter words, horizontally and vertically.

Numerous commercial games have been based on the cross-word. The British Museum Catalogue lists a game called *Crossword Golf*. Unfortunately, the Museum's copy of the game has been lost and one can only speculate on how this mysterious game was played. Most enduring of the various board games inspired by the crossword is the ingenious *Scrabble*. The first sets were issued about 1948, although the rules were subsequently slightly revised in 1953. At least two books have been devoted to the game and are worth seeking out, if only because they include the rules for Scrabblegram – a version of the game for one player.

In 1970, journalist Gyles Brandreth was visiting Bristol Prison – to do some research, not as a guest of Her Majesty – when he noticed a couple of inmates playing *Scrabble*. This brought home to him that it isn't purely a middle-class game but is played by all manner of people. It wasn't long before he felt it was high time that Scrabblers were given the opportunity to stand even with chess players and bridge enthusiasts by having a National Championship of their own. He placed an advertisement in several newspapers, expecting a few dozen replies. Three days later with over a thousand enquiries, he had a national championship to organise.

The eliminating round for the championship involves contestants playing a couple of games at home and submitting their scores to the organising committee. The hundred top scorers are then invited to play a series of games at a London Hotel. Scrabble Champion in 1973 was Mrs. Anne Bradford of Barnet – Anne was also among the finalists of the *Cutty Sark/Times* Crossword Championship. Average *Scrabble* players can amass a total of about 250 points in twenty or so goes. In six goes of her final game in the contest, Mrs. Bradford had already passed 300. One word alone gave her the astonishing score of 149. Using such rare but approved (invigilated by the Chief Editor of the Oxford English Dictionaries) words as ort, ai, ria and oyers, Anne ended with a mind-blowing 1266.

Recently, the Greater London Scrabble League (which fields three divisions of Scrabble teams) produced a useful list of permitted two-letter words:

ad, ae, ai, am, an, at, as, ax, ay, be, bo, by da, do, ea, eh, el, em, en, er, es, ex, fa, fy, go, gu, ha, he, hi, ho, id, if, in, io, is, it, jo, ka, ky, la, li, lo, ma, me, mi, mo, my, na, no, ob, od, oe, of, oh, on, oo, or, ow, ox, oy, pa, pi, re, sh, si, st, so, ta, te, ti, to, un, up, ur, ut, us, we, wo, ye, yo, yu, and zo.

This list is not all-inclusive. Certainly, it doesn't incorporate CH, PH, SH, and ST, all of which are in *Chambers' Dictionary*. PH is particularly attractive: properly speaking, it should be pH, a term used in chemistry. As Darryl Francis and Richard Francis pointed out in an article in the monthly magazine *Games & Puzzles*, official Scrabble rules prevent you from using words starting with capital letters – but they don't say anything about capitals at the end!

Figure Words is a simple word-building game for the family. It was invented by crossword compiler F. G. Dulley and first appeared in his book *Crosswords for You* in 1947.

In playing a four-handed game, each player takes one of the squares below and a copy of the letter value chart. Each letter of the alphabet has a numerical value.

Each player builds up his or her own square, using ingenuity in introducing words which will result in the highest number of points, but remember that words down have to be fitted into words across. Mark off completed words by a thick line.

No word must be used more than once. Points are allowed only for letters in completed words; so letters can, in fact, score twice, i.e., once in a completed word across and once in a completed word down.

LETTER VALUE CHART

A	B	C	D	E	F	G	H	I	J	K	L	M
3	6	8	8	3	10	9	6	4	10	7	12	14

N	O	P	Q	R	S	T	U	V	W	X	Y	Z
10	5	11	20	7	5	7	6	10	13	11	8	18

11. Solving Them and Setting Them

As in most arts, practice makes perfect. The inexperienced solver soon learns to scan his clues, hoping to gain even single letters to place on his empty crossword grid. If he finds a clue that implies a plural ending, he tentatively puts an S in the last box of the appropriate answer. A third person singular ending of a verb will likewise suggest an S in the last box. Past tense verb endings will encourage him to write down an ED. Participate verb endings: ING. Comparative adjectives: ER or EST. That's a start. It might at least generate the first letter of a connecting word. If the number of letters in clue is the same as in the solution, he considers the possibility that it might be an anagram. After that he's on his own, struggling day by day to become familiar with the type of clue favoured by the journal he is currently using.

Or he can call on outside aid. His first purchase must obviously be a good dictionary. Preferably *Chambers' Twentieth Century Dictionary*, seeing as this is the one employed by most compilers – thanks to its bold-type printing of composite terms, inflections and figures of speech. For the wealthier solver, the two-volume or four-volume editions of the *Shorter Oxford Dictionary* given even greater capacity to travel the byways of the English language. If he really wants to go to town, there are always the twenty-four majestic volumes of *The Oxford English Dictionary*. *Roget's Thesaurus* and *The Oxford Dictionary of Quotations* come next on the shopping list. Less well-known than it should be is *Walker's Rhyming Dictionary*. This book works in a curious way. In a conventional dictionary, you find a particular word by first looking for the initial letter, then the second letter, and so on. *Walker's* operates in reverse, entries being listed according to the letters at the end of the word. Words ending in AA are followed by words ending in BA, then CA, and so on. Very useful if you have discovered one or two terminal letters to an answer but are defeated by the clue.

Beyond these, the more reference books the better. A set of Shakespeare, a good Bible concordance, a set of encyclopaedias, a dictionary of dates and an atlas won't go amiss.

The crossword craze was scarcely under way before alert publishers hit on the idea of assembling special reference dictionaries to aid solvers. Dictionaries of this type are still available – most large bookshops should be able to show you several titles.

The Complete Crossword Reference Book edited by N. St. Barbe Sladen is published by Pearson and dates back to 1932, when it was first prepared by C. H. R. Thorn. It lists words alphabetically within groups of equal word length. The idea is that if you are seeking a six-letter word beginning with TA, instead of going through all the TA's in a normal dictionary, you can save time by just scanning the TA's in the section of six-letter words. This book also gives valuable lists of words in approximately two hundred categories such as 'Some boy's schools'; 'Surgical terms'; 'Literary characters of Dickens' (and 27 other authors); and 'Makes of motor-car'. Well, did *you* know there was a car called the Rockne and one by the name of Figone?

Chambers' Crossword Aid edited by D. F. A. Michael is published by Chambers and is based on their *Twentieth Century Dictionary*. Again, this lists words according to the number of letters, going up to twelve-letter words. Where else could you find 108 words of only two letters each?

The Crossword Companion by 'M.R.W.' is published by Herbert Jenkins and has a mere 52 two-letter words. Even the puzzle compiler's old friend, the Sun-God Ra, fails to put in an appearance. On the other hand, its listing of words includes words of eighteen letters, nineteen letters and even one twenty-letter specimen: philoprogenitiveness.

Each specialised dictionary has its merits. So inspect two or three to see which suits you best. The latest addition to the field, a *Private Eye* publication, has the dramatic title of *The Crossword Computer*.

One interesting guide, long out of print, is the *Sporting Record Crossword Pointer*. This book assumes you have at hand *The Concise Oxford Dictionary*, *Nuttall's Standard Dictionary* and *Chambers' Twentieth Century Dictionary*. If you are checking on the meaning, or even the existence, of an unfamiliar word, the guide tells you which of these dictionaries, if any, will include it. It works like this:

CO refers to the *Concise Oxford Dictionary*
Ad refers to the Addenda of that dictionary
N refers to *Nuttall's Standard Dictionary*
C refers to *Chambers' Twentieth Century Dictionary*
Sp refers to the Supplement of *Nuttall's* or *Chambers'*
An asterisk in any column means that the word is listed in this dictionary as a separate entry.

	CO	Ad	N	Sp	C	Sp
SUFI	★				-SM	
FEHME					V-	
JANUS	★		★		-ARY	
MANTY					-UA	
SKART					-C-F	

Thus, SUFI will be found in the *Concise Oxford*, is missing from *Nuttall's* and will be found under SUFISM in *Chambers'*.

FEHME can be found only in Chambers' in the entry beginning VEHM-. If you look this up, you'll discover the word VEHMGERICHT.

JANUS is in the *Concise Oxford* and *Nuttall's*. In *Chambers'* it comes under JANUARY.

MANTY appears only in *Chambers'*. Look under MANTUA.

SKART is also restricted to *Chambers'* under its alternative spelling, SCARF.

The *Sporting Record Crossword Pointer* was designed to aid competitors in alternative-choice crossword competitions. Here the answer to a clue is, in effect, often a word with one letter missing – with a choice of several letters to fit the answer. Suppose your clue is 'This doesn't last very long' and the four-letter answer is -ORM. CORM, FORM and WORM suggest themselves immediately. The guide, however, also reveals the existence of NORM and GORM. GORM, it turns out, is only in Nuttall's and means the excessive shine on new varnish. It is reasonable to assume that this must be the correct solution. Using this remarkable guide, the whole search for this word takes only a matter of seconds. Quite remarkable.

Once you've solved a clue, can you ever be absolutely sure you have the solution intended by the compiler? That was a question that must have bothered Herbert Atherton of Wimbledon for he came up with an answer in 1930. He wanted compilers to add a figure in brackets after the clue. For instance, 'Girl's name (50)'. This was before compilers had developed the habit of placing in brackets the number of letters in the answer. Mr. Atherton's number was derived from adding together the numerical values of each letter in the solution . . . A being equal to 1, B = 2, C = 3, and so on.

$$\begin{array}{ccccc} E & T & H & E & L \\ 5 & 20 & 8 & 5 & 12 \end{array} \quad \text{Total: 50}$$

Once you think you have a correct solution to a clue, you simply add up the numerical values and see if you get the same value as the compiler. The inventor of the idea presumably hoped to earn a royalty from it as he took the precaution of printing it as a leaflet and depositing it in the British Museum to establish his copyright. The system was never used in Britain although the same idea has been employed in the United States.

Now, how to set a crossword. Clearly, you need a grid diagram. Convention dictates that it should be symmetrical, unless you are thinking of an unusual specialised puzzle. (Torquemada's masterpieces were hardly ever symmetrical. His successor in *The Observer*, Ximenes, opted for symmetry, occasionally making a slight deviation if he faced such complications as the inclusion of long words.)

How many black squares should there be in proportion to how many white squares (or 'lights' as they are properly called)? This

131

depends on the proportion of 'unchecked' letters you intend to include. A letter is checked when it contributes both to an across word and a down word. In early crosswords every letter was checked. This meant that you could complete a solution to the crossword simply by solving the across words, or alternatively just the down words. Apart from making solving far too easy, it forced the compiler into using too many short words. Very boring. Hence the popularity of the gnu, the emu and good old Ra. Such crosswords died a quick death in Britain – except for those printed in children's papers – but this type of crossword is still the most widely used in the United States. What do I hear you say? Those compilers ought to be in prison. As a matter of fact, they are. Of the one hundred compilers who supply crosswords to two New York puzzle magazines, twenty-five are behind bars!

In the ideal diagram at least half the letters in the diagram should be checked. Say, between 55% and 75%. No word should be completely checked. Furthermore, at least half the letters of every word should be checked. Otherwise, you don't give the solver a reasonable chance. To quote Ximenes in his book *Ximenes on the Art of the Crossword*, 'If, after having filled in all the interlocking words, they are left with something like -A-E-, there are so many possibilities that even a fairish but somewhat elusive clue may fail to suggest the answer in reasonable time, and the solver has fair grounds for feeling dissatisfied.' It is also considered not to be playing the game to face the solver with two or three consecutive unchecked letters in a word. An analysis of the different types of grid pattern is given in *Anatomy of the Crossword* by D. St. P. Barnard, a *Daily Telegraph* compiler.

Now you need to fill up the grid. You'll note some interesting things as you go along. You'll realise that while short words end with a considerable variety of letters, medium and long words don't. They tend to finish with a surprisingly small choice of terminal letters: E, D, H, L, N, R, S, T, W and Y. This is why a puzzle's least inspired words are usually grouped at the base and right hand sides. Words like 'endless', 'tested' and 'seeders'. That's only one problem. Another one is the frequent need for vowels in the middle of words, or appearing in groups. Which explains the frequency of such tired old clichés as aardvark, Aaron, Baal, uniak and Taa.

Finally, the clues. Everyone is familiar with the simple definition clue and the anagram. But these are only the small arms in the cluesmith's weaponry. Barnard's book lists the cryptic definition, the allusion, the dialectic clue, the dilemmatic clue, the paragram, the disjunctive clue and the parabolic clue. The best advice I can give is to say: get hold of Barnard's book *Anatomy of the Crossword* and *Ximenes on the Crossword* by D. S. Macnutt. Each book gives a rare opportunity to see how a formidable brain applies itself to the creative process. A sample from *Ximenes on the Crossword*:

> IN—S. Inns and Inks aren't easy to make interesting: what about the Spanish name Ines, given in that wonderful list of 'The More Common English Christian Names' in *Chambers*. Wasn't there a famous one? Look up the name in *Brewer's Reader's Handbook*. We find she was the mother of Don Juan, and wanted to make her son a model of all the virtues. 'Wanted her child to become a model?' is pleasantly misleading (towards a daughter) and at the same time fair. Now what about the subsidiary? After much cogitation, we decide to look up words ending in -iness in the rhyming dictionary, with a view to using a word that contains her. 'Dreaminess' can be connected with her dreams about her son's future: 'Had dreams about her in reverie' (dream-Ines-s) continues to mislead towards a girl. Alter the first part to 'Could her child become a model?' and we have a perfectly fair but difficult clue. (That, incidentally, has taken twenty-five minutes, almost as long as the other five put together: that's how it goes.)

A few words of advice in case you do try compiling crosswords and eventually see them into print:

1. Check your handwriting. Jack Luzzato, a puzzle compiler in New York for over forty years, constructed a puzzle including

the word DOPE. When he came to make up the clues some time later, he misread his writing and mistook the D for a P. The definition he made up was 'Catholic chief'. Luzzato's description of the public reaction: 'The bombs really fell.'

2. Check your spelling. Mistakes are found most frequently in the down words. Reason? The eye doesn't like reading vertically. So your eye doesn't notice if you've spelled ELOIT for ELIOT.

3. Don't use the wrong diagram. No kidding. It happens. In 1958, *Time & Tide* printed the right clues but the wrong diagram. A substantial number of readers actually managed to solve the clues, reconstruct the diagram and submit their correct solutions! And it wasn't an easy crossword in the first place. The Editor printed this protest from one reader:

> Blimey, fellas, 'ere's a do!
> Never heard the like, 'ave you?
> 'Tain't enough the clues to bust—
> Gotta work the squares out fust!

4. Check your facts. A paper in Richmond, Virginia, gave this clue: 'Confederate General'. The answer was Grant. Now considering what Grant did to Richmond, you'd think they could get that one right!

12. Some Favourites

This chapter is an indulgence on the part of the author and includes examples of crosswords that have given him particular pleasure. The first three are from H. E. Dudeney's book 'The World's Best Word Puzzles', published in 1925, and represent the first attempts to break away from the conventional crossword format.

PUZZLE No. 39
'The Alphabet' by H. E. Dudeney
Although very simple to solve, this is probably the only crossword of its type ever published.

The point of this little crossword is that every one of the twenty-six letters of the alphabet is used once and only once. We give the definitions, but do not indicate the locations of the words or their direction, horizontal or vertical.

DEFINITIONS
A metal. Parts of trees. To annoy.
Whim or imagination. A sign,
example. What person or persons.
A man's shortened Christian name.
To puzzle or, make sport of.

'The British Lion' by H. E. Dudeney

Designed in 1925, this is one of the first crosswords to use an unconventional shape. The absence of black squares makes this type of puzzle very easy for the solver – but difficult for the compiler.

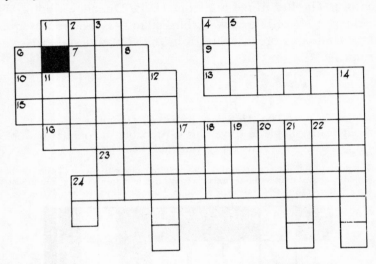

DEFINITIONS – HORIZONTALS

All the other squares have to be filled

1. A number.
4. Location.
7. An animal.
9. That is.
10. A favourite dish with Scotsmen.
13. A madman.
15. To check.
16. One at home with the world.
23. Dependants.
24. Definite.

VERTICALS

2. A black man.
3. The letters of 'EEL PEGS' in disorder.
4. Object.
5. A beverage.
6. An exclamation.
8. Fate, destiny.
11. Where St. Joan came from.
12. Those who throw stones.
14. Agreement.
17. A postscript with initial.
18. Two vowels followed by a consonant.
19. A joint of mutton or pork curtailed.
20. For travellers.
21. To worry.
22. Dexterity.
24. Perform.

PUZZLE No. 41

An attractive little puzzle designed by H. E. Dudeney in 1925

We give the definitions of all the words, but do not indicate their locations or directions, horizontal or vertical. At the foot we give all the twenty-five letters used. As all except four are three-letter words, it is not difficult to find a good many probable words and then try fitting them together, but good guesses at the five-letter words will be very helpful.

A A A A C
C E E E E
I I N N O
P R R S S
T T T W W

DEFINITIONS

Expression of grief. A domestic animal.
A disturbance. A youth. Mimic. A line.
Rents. Cold. A punishment. A trap.
A lover. An animal. Worn on the head.
A table delicacy.

Readers who can remember *The Strand Magazine* and *John O' London's Weekly* will recall the delightful mathematical, inferential and word puzzles that appeared in these journals. These were the creation of W. T. Williams and G. H. Savage. Savage was a Cambridge graduate in mathematics, and was for many years a master at Wellington, an Inspector of Schools and examiner for the Civil Service Commission. Williams was educated at University College, Aberystwyth, and also took up schoolmastering, spending most of his life teaching English Literature. The author of several editions of English Classics for school use, he initiated the literary competitions which were a feature of *John O' London's Weekly* and conducted these under the pseudonym of 'Tantalus'. For many years he was also the editor of 'Perplexities' in the *Strand Magazine*. The following puzzles give an indication of the inventiveness of this duet of problemists.

PUZZLE No. 42

'Crossword Surprise'

This puzzle and the following two are from *The Penguin Problems Book* by W. T. Williams and G. H. Savage – published in 1940.

1	2	3	4	5	6	7	8
9				10			
11				12			
13				14			
15	16	17	18	19	20	21	22
23				24			
25				26			
27				28			

ACROSS

1. Burrowing animal.
5. Body of musicians.
9. Breakwater.
10. Form into a league.
11. Blemish on human skin.
12. Fillet.
13. Its hills make mountains.
14. Full of Hope it abstains.
15. Piece of tobacco.
19. Obligation.
23. Vulgar sovereign.
24. Tax.
25. What Caesar asked.
26. Respect.
27. Twenty-fifth of a pony.
28. Customs.

DOWN

1. Printers' measures.
2. Is indebted.
3. Measures taken when given inches.
4. Facility.
5. Insects.
6. Quite indefinite articles.
7. Half of one down.
8. Four pence.
15. Tails.
16. Employ.
17. Affirmative voters.
18. Two doctors of divinity.
19. Add up to 2,000.
20. Handle.
21. Annoy.
22. Sage.

PUZZLE No. 43

'Mr. Turtle'

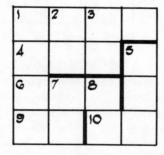

Fragments of the late Mr. Turtle's life history are embodied (or embedded) in the following numerical 'crossword':

ACROSS

1. The year when Mr. Turtle was born.
4. Nine times Mr. Turtle's age when his youngest grandchild, Bert, was born 'in the first sennight of some smiling May.'
6. Eleven times the number of Mr. Turtle's grandchildren.
9. Mr. Turtle's age at the time of his decease, Lady Day, 1934.
10. The square root of Mr. Turtle's birth-year.

DOWN

1. The cube of the number of Mr. Turtle's natal day in November.
2. The number of Mr. Turtle's residence in Balmoral Avenue.
3. Age attained by Mr. Turtle in the Diamond Jubilee Year.
5. Bert's age, in days, when Grandpa died.
7. Mr. Turtle's age at the outbreak of the Great War.
8. Mr. Turtle's lucky number.

139

1	2	3	4	5	6	4	7	4
2	6	2	■	2	■	8	4	5
9	■	7	2	8	4	2	■	4
7	2	4	■	4	■	3	7	1
■	5	■	5	6	2	■	9	■
3	4	0	■	2	■	3	4	0
2	■	6	2	9	1	4	■	7
0	6	2	■	1	■	1	6	4
6	2	7	1	4	1	6	2	4

PUZZLE No. 44

'A Crossword in Code'

The ten letters which have been used in this crossword are represented by the digits 0 to 9. Twenty of the twenty-eight words formed by these ten letters appear actually in the following storyette, while the remaining eight are indicated by clues in italics. The positions of the words are to be discovered by the reader:

A popular novelist is *part author* of a story the scene of which is laid somewhere in the East, in *a land which is the reverse of the mode* to-day. Here the hero arrived in a Moth 'plane – to which a lucky horseshoe had been attached – and soon he met the inevitable 'she', who was feeding her ewes in the pastoral manner of that land. His first gasp of 'Oh' was unoriginal, tho' his second 'Ho, Ho', and his further 'Oho' and *confused 'Hems'* were even more so. Later at the house of a rather sour widow, Mrs. Roe – *concerning whom the authors tell us little except that her horsemanship was reminiscent of a *cowboy exhibition*, and that her family tree was impressive – affection ripened. We owe the authors a grudge for a cynical ending, for after our hero and heroine were *wed*, *contrarily* enough, both were inclined to *regret* their bargain.

PUZZLE No. 45

'My First Motor Cycle'

The Second Penguin Problems Book by Williams and Savage, 1944, provides this puzzle and the following two.

Its registration number, 1 *ac.*, was the product of three primes, 7 *ac.* being one, and 6 *ac.* the product of the other two. I bought it one summer for 2 *down* pounds; my age at the time, multiplied by the number of years it remained in my possession, is the number obtained by dividing 8 *ac.* by a certain prime. The date?

Well, if you multiply the year by the square root of one-tenth of 1 *down*, and then add 1 *down*, you get 5 *ac.* That's clear, I hope.

When Great War No. 1 was a year old, I sold the machine for 9 *ac.* pounds – one-third of its cost. It had a light petrol consumption; its miles-per-gallon number (a multiple of 9 *ac.*) was just one-nineteenth of 5 *down*. If 4 *down* is the cube of a factor of 1 *ac.*, and 3 *down* is the square of nine times 6 *ac.*, and my birthday is in December, how old was I in February, 1941?

141

PUZZLE No. 46

'Cross-Number Puzzle'

No number is duplicated. There are four cube and three square numbers in the puzzle. 1 *down* is a square. 1 *across* is a prime factor of 5 *across* and of 3 *down*. 7 *across*, whose digits add up to fifteen, is the product of 1 *across* and 9 *across*. 4 *across*, which is a factor of 6 *down*, is one less than 5 *across*.

PUZZLE No. 47

'Cross-Number Roman'

ACROSS

1. H.C.F. of 3 across and 3 down.
3. Difference of 3 down and 1 across.
5. Ten times 1 across + square of 2 down.
6. A square (reversed).
8. Difference of 1 across and 2 down.

DOWN

1. 1 across × 2 down.
2. A square.
3. 1 across × 4 down.
4. Half the square root of product of 6 across (reversed) and 2 down.
6. 2 down × 7 down.
7. Sum of 3 across and 3 down, divided by 1 across.

142

So many British magazines and newspapers publish good crosswords that it seems invidious to single any particular publication as a favourite. Nevertheless, the weekly news magazine *Time & Tide* maintains a continually high standard and occasionally excels beyond expectations, as with the following two puzzles both dating from 1958. The first reflects the journal's right-wing political leanings. In the second one, by the same compiler, you are given two identical squares. The narrative provides sufficient squares to fill in the two. That is, each number occurs twice in the narrative, but no indication is given as to the square in which the answer is to be set. You are left to sort out that choice!

PUZZLE No. 48

'The New 13 Across Movement'
A *Time and Tide* crossword by Valcol.

We are told that the workers are not **26** (2-9), that lack of effort **13** *down* output, and that that's what's **1** *down* with things today. Well, this is a Welfare State, isn't it? Why should we worry about the good of **28** at large, so long as nothing goes **24** for us, and there's plenty in the **19** (3, 7)? Why give more in labour than you need? The worker no longer **5** *down* (6, 3) in hand, cowed before the master, nor does he have to worry, pinch and **16** (6, 2) he holds steady to his own **25** in the new (be geologic, and call it **18**, if you like) **13** *across* movement, **13** *across* that is to excessive labour. It gives results throughout the country **7** (2, 5), Wigan or **1** *across*. No need of force, strikes or **22**; work to rule, and take it easy, **17** effort. Make use of the **6**, but let the officials understand who calls the tune these days. Be a member of the **26** (2-9) **28**, but use it for your own good. **12** up as a success any move that adds to the **19** (3, 7). Have no delicate promptings of conscience such as Robert **20** felt, that novel young clergyman of Victorian days, nor seek to live the ascetic life of the old-time **21**. We are no longer 'rude **10** that work for bread; even if ours should happen to be **23** (1, 8) employment, our thoughts are set on those higher things, the car and the 'telly'. We're no longer to be classed as **5** *across*. We know what's what and how to get it.

England's is a **11** (5, 4), and a pleasant one. So let's do the best for ourselves at home. Why worry about **11** or China? let who will complain that we spin out our **2** drinking the good old drop of cha – no **4** for us then, if your please. Not one of us sets up as a **3** with a progressive outlook. Ours is a partisan policy, and will bring us no **9** (1, 1, 1) award, Scandals there may be among the **6** what of the executive council of the **27** (1, 1, 1) with its election wangle and all that? Justification can no doubt be found **7** (2, 5) or some other historian for condemning such a movement **14** (2, 1, 6), a creeping paralysis in the body politic. Many long for the strict authority that the **29** once exercised in Carthage, or for the absolute power, say, of the Macedonian general, **8**, who defeated the Gauls. Such people are not for the workers' **25**. Fascists I call them. But more of this **15**. We'll make money, while the going's good.

Chambers' Twentieth Century Dictionary, New Mid-Century Version, is recommended

PUZZLE No. 49

'Venture into Space' by Valcol – a double crossword from Time & Tide

The two squares given are identical, and the narrative provides sufficient clues to fill the two. That is, each number occurs twice in the narrative, but no indication is given as to the square in which the answer is to be set. The solver is left to sort out that problem.

I do not wish to 7 or deceive you in this account of my 28 in space, worthy, as they are, to be set beside those of 22, but it would be difficult to 6 (4; 1; 4) in space-fiction more packed with extraordinary adventures. My story, like that 1 *down* (2; 6), is a true one, and might, like his, be entitled in Latin 18 (4; 8). For I too 'humbly solicit my readers' incredulity', when 'I now make the only true statement you are to expect – that I am a liar'. It has too some of the 27 and imagination that characterises other well-known tales. The shades of famous inventors such as Marconi, 21 and 28 (Auguste, of cinematographic renown) might indeed pale at this mechanised exploit of a later day. Now that I am back on solid earth, it 17 and appals me to think of what we passed through, and I would that I had, to do my account justice, the art of that old rhetorician, 'honey-tongued' 21 who wrote On Providence and Divine Manifestations.

It all started one evening in the New 19 5 *down* when I met my great friend, 10 (7; 4) Jun., son of the globe-encircling sire. He proposed that I accompany him and his father's valet 18 on what he called 15 Moonraker. He had a space-ship, newly built, somewhat on the lines of a war-time 16, one of those used for escorting convoys, which he had named 1 *across*

after the air-borne steed. So it was that without 15 preparation we departed one night, I bidding farewell to my wife 9 and 18 to a blonde he abbreviatedly addressed as 9 (or little) 9. We were immediately 3 (2; 3), and found ourselves 14 (2; 3; 2; 3; 2), feeling at first I imagine very much like 1 *down* when he drove off with his father's car. We had certainly followed a novel precedent, and were 2 (4; 4) the wind. The route ran broad and plain ahead, comparable, say, to the 13 (6; 4), the King's highway of Spain in America and the American dramatist's play. We encountered practically no traffic 1 *across* or incoming. Our movement could not be described as 27; we travelled fast, and soon 4 (6; 4) a flying island, probably 19, which is spoken of in 22's 28. So on to our first stop, the moon, where we suitably 7 for a while, taking stock of the terrain.

On Aldebaran which we next visited we found in a hut, much reassembling a 5 *down* of the Orkneys, what we thought might be traces of the lost 20, Electra, one 12 and her slumber-wear, a 8; perhaps she'd forgotten to pack them after a visit. On another star we spotted the tracks of some beast, the prints possibly of that mysterious creature, 14 (2; 10) 5 *across*, yet I, though that sounds

146

much like giving a clue, have my doubts. We did not see it, but had a clear view of a bird that much resembled the 24 of Wonderland. The Milky Way put on a dazzling show, worthy to rank with Son et 28, bedewed and 12, as it was, with dancing particles of starry dust, but one of the most marvellous sights in our voyaging was the crystal bridge 25 (7; 4), that lyric star, to 16, the beehive cluster in Cancer. It arched mystic and bright above the dark void 23, wherein we travelled beneath.

There were on Betelgeuse inhabitants, housed in 5 *across*, although not dead; yet they were not in a sense alive, but wrapt in unnaturally deep sleep or 3. We were 11 from landing on Procyon by rough weather, but on 16 had a pleasant little conversation or 17 with 'a gordian shape of dazzling hue', 23, though she was inclined to 24 one a little too much for heart's ease. A contrary wind, blowing up 14 (2; 10) fog, also 11 our intention to bring our 1 *across* to land on 1 *across*, where we had been told that 9ith, Adam's first wife, still lives. Appropriately enough we heard some of the music of the spheres on Lyra, where folk were assembled to 25 (4; 2; 5), a concert hall, for future use. The 20 had been engaged to sing in

celebration of the occasion; their strains fell most ravishingly on the 26. There was also a set 6 (2; 7 – if you prefer that word) of seven harpists whose skill was transcendent, whether they played scherzando, 27 or doloroso. But the climax of our voyaging was the 4 (5; 5) entertainment to which we were treated on the Evening Star, 10 (1; 10) after the good old Roman fashion, such 1 *across*-s, such fun and games. Hercules had been engaged with his 5 to keep some sort of order – no other restraint on the merry-making. The food and drink were excellent; we were given 22 to enable us to draw ambrosia and nectar *ad lib.*, though the indigenous revellers were more partial to 26 or sesame and edible 8 obtained from the meadows bordering a near-by lake, about the size of the 2 sea.

After this junketing, as we had now reached an unconscionable height, and discretion had not entirely 2 (4; 4) our increasing exaltation 3 (2; 3), it seemed wise 13 (3; 7) to return to earth, and so I will 15 no further. On the seventh day after setting out we landed safely in America in the state of 11. Now, having enjoyed such commerce with the celestials, we must 19 our ways and revert to mundane living.

147

No collection of crosswords could be complete without a specimen of the work of Afrit. A headmaster, as well as Prebendary of Wells Cathedral, A. F. Ritchie invented many specialist types of crossword, including the 'Playfair' puzzle in which a number of answers are concealed by using the Playfair code – a cipher device first developed for the transmission of secret messages. The Afrit puzzle included here certainly doesn't indicate the compiler at his most difficult, but has been selected for its curiosity value – note the self-portrait of the compiler.

PUZZLE No. 50

'Afrit' by Afrit

One of A. F. Ritchie's finest puzzles from *The Listener*. The diagram represents a self-portrait of the compiler, with the Q's as eyes.

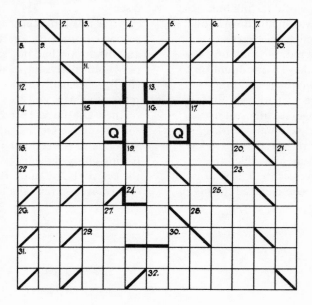

ACROSS

2. Advice about German, as you might expect from Afrit.
8. Tree of Afrit's country providing some protection from the weather.
11. Afrit has been constrained to do so to the Commander of the Faithful to show ill-feeling about him.
12. Afrit delights in games like this.
13. But in a game like this he is more at home.
14. Pitch-queerer of Taj-el-Rekah, etc.
18. Bridegroom only incidentally celebrated by Afrit.
19. Urchin of the same element as Sinbad's Old Man.
22. Tropical ruminant which according to Afrit's ruminations would be more numerous if the river turned to ice.
23. Flowed peacock-green between another pseudonymous 'Man of Words' and his Lombard landlady lady-love.
24. Pilot whose part Afrit sometimes plays when his head is turned.
26. Owing to Morgiana's Ali Baba's was rendered doubtful once more.
28. Catkin from country almost within Afrit's sphere of influence.
29. On his tomb in Arabian tale was 'The Tree of the Bridegroom and Bride'.
31. Supernatural-seeming but un mythological gold coins.
32. Hairy fellow, as the Jinn might say of Afrit.

DOWN

1. Extinct Muscovite militiaman partially kindled anew.
3. Sister of a temporary swan not of Afrit's mythology.
4. Decidedly feminine in spite of the masculine element.
5. Tail-twisting is sure to, as this tail-twisted tail-twister did the English fleet.
6. Headless rodent, is shorter and lots longer when cetaceous.
7. Member of Slaughter House who remained faithful to Notley's while Biggs and Berry fought.
9. Tree whose initial and final interchange shows no easy connection with Afrit's opposite.
10. On its plural shrieking peasants 'fell down in terror' at the apparition of a walking but incomplete suit of clothes.
15. Tree which would have served Mr. H. G. Wells equally well as the title of one of his tales of wonder.
16. Part of a coat with a tail whose first five you may.
17. Spot of ulceration like that removed from horse's eye in Arabian tale.
20. Dainty provided by a god up-river.
21. Correctly named by supposedly insane young prince to whom Afrit had brought an unconscious princess by night.
25. Mythological Eve apparently just as blameworthy as her Biblical counterpart.
27. Its 'genuine sense' is its, but usually it has on more.
30. 'You never know whether it is the day when he can pronounce his "r's".'

149

This crossword was drawn to my attention in the book *Ximenes on the Art of the Crossword*. In 1925 *The Daily News* ran a crossword contest with a first prize of £5,000. A hundred thousand readers entered the first round of the contest. Gilbert Frankau, the novelist, was then called in to produce a series of four puzzles of increasing difficulty. Three hundred competitors solved the third of these, but no complete solution was received for the final puzzle. The prize was shared by a syndicate of readers having the smallest number of errors.

PUZZLE No. 51

Gilbert Frankau's Contest Puzzle for the Evening Standard

ACROSS

1. Initialise a father.
202. By adding hydrogen here, help the British Dyestuffs Corporation.
303. Full of hops.
404. Curtail a formula.
5. Might describe the condition of a rustic wooer.
6. A poetess.
7. A moke.
8. The guns of Trafalgar.
9. Curtail and decapitate an enormous oven.
10. Reverse one part of a pulley block.
11. One way out of the harem
12. Once decapitate and thrice curtail the race of a man whose skin might have been saved had he been able to exercise 11 across.
13. Decapitate and curtail something which also answers to clue 44 across.
14. Curtail and decapitate that which apparently did *not* fall.
15. Twice curtail an exiguous meadow.
16. Two code letters found on a certain brand of advertised cigarettes.
17. Reverse either three-fourths or three-fifths of a neurosis.
18. Add one and make a tragedy.
19. Curtail and decapitate a diminutive.
20. Her husband's initials were J. R.
21. Found under the table.
22. Reverse two words which might describe the influence of several specimens on the judgment of a mining engineer.
23. First reverse, then twice decapitate an idler.
24. Look for this on the end of a blowpipe.
25. Reverse one thorough paced scoundrel.
26. Reverse something made of chestnuts.
27. First reverse, then twice decapitate a city bossed by a bull.
28. Might describe hawthorn.
29. Curtail a Saracen's stronghold.
30. Curtail a word associated with mice.
31. First reverse, then invert the first two letters of a knowledge invaluable to Mr. Royce.
32. Ask your tailor about this.
33. Found under expensive cigar boxes.
34. Could also be initialised as U, Q, F, E, G, D.

35. See house agents' advertisements.
36. Start an ode.
37. Curtail one who would have been better shingled.
38. The fore-runner of the land girl.
39. Twice curtail that which put behind 72 across conveys social reform.
40. By decapitation and the alteration of one letter, make print vocal.
41. One of the lacertilia.
42. Reverse the first half of a hill.
43. A form of promotion.
44. Dished up with vegetables.
45. A female.
46. Add a couple and make a row.
47. To surround.
48. Curtail a village.
49. Set our fathers singing.
50. Curtail one who goes veiled.
51. Made men cry, 'Bring out your dead'.
52. A relative of Peeping Tom.
53. One who entered on behalf of the House.
54. Curtail a river.
55. Might have been the first two words of a historic South African cable.
56. Remove two letters from contracts.
57. ⎫ By combining these two make a
57a. ⎭ lark.
58. Decapitate a doubtful beautifier.
59. Reverse a form of communication.
60. Two-thirds of a military unit.
61. Deduct an aromatic liquid from an aromatic plant.
62. B.C. three thousand two hundred and sixty.
63. Gives knights nightmare.
64. Reverse projections.
65. The last of the fairies.
66. Curtail an inhabitant of the Gebbi.
67. Singularise and reverse a reversal.
68. First decapitate, then reverse a property vital to a play.
69. Twice beheaded a fearsome monster.
70. Nice nickname (reversed) for a brace of peeresses.
71. Once decapitate and thrice curtail a business which is also an art.
72. See 39 across.
73. A chorus.

151

DOWN

1. Title of a poem.
40. Seven score.
55. Reverse that which makes men distrust legality.
2. The novice oarsman's friend.
3. Halve a frisky lady.
4. Reverse a process Biblically connected with a beard.
5. An appellation of intimacy.
606. Would apply to 21 across.
7. Reverse a sign of decomposition.
38. Reverse a name.
39. A great handicap.
8. The answer the doctor made to his nagging wife.
9. Makes H. G. Wells see red.
10. Reverse an inflammation.
11. Reverse whom you curse.
12. Thrice curtail a trade-mark.
13. Reverse that which has as bad an effect as 9 down.
14. Curtail a cereal.
15. Cross.
16. Reverse a revenue payer.
202. Reverse a patient carrier.
203. A racecourse.
59. Depenultimise an African tribe.
204. The first two letters of 303 across.
205. Stops 'fans' fanning.
206. More trouble for H. G. Wells.
44. Reverse a newspaper suggestion about 46 across.
207. Half a fruit.
208. Appeal to peelers.
209. Leslie Henson does this.
210. Reverse an obsolescent individual.
211. Several Zevs.
212. What the Yorkshireman said when they offered him ginger beer.
213. Reverse, then four times decapitate a war policy.
214. The day to which no one looks forward.
215. Reverse a flapper's dream.
216. Curtail that which tallies with 40 across.
217. Initialise and reverse a preserver (?) of morality.
57a. A monopoly.
218. Reverse a headman.

303. Reverse a phrase which might be used by a Channel swimmer.
304. Halve embellished.
305. Stand a cup on its rim.
306. Halve a cake.
307. Bad in the lung, worse in the brain.
308. Deduct first an American animal, then an English interjection from a barometrical term. Then reverse your result.
309. Add a conveyance and make a spectacle.
310. One of these rarely obtains 311 down.
311. Rarely obtained by 310 down.
312. Reverse a knight.
313. Another Wells.
314. Give this to your enemies.
315. Curtail and reverse a provider of transport.
316. Reverse the last two letters of 55 across.
317. Reverse three primal liquids.
404. First deduct the opposition from, then reverse a word whose original significance is precisely the opposite of opposition.
405. Sets Chinamen gobbling.
406. The wrong way to pluralise some Orientals.
37. The gardener's friend.
407. Not the Southern's, we hope.
408. First reverse then decapitate the forerunner of 55 down.
409. Add the beginning and the end of 65 across to the ultimate of 1 across and the penultimate of 71 across.
410. A reformer.
51. Curtail a kicker.
411. Was used for keening.
412. Reverse a sign of utility.
47. Initialise a story title.
413. One of the things that is his.
414. Reverse the first half of a Swinburnian town.
415. Reverse and add a couple to 317 down.
415a. Voyage, and learn this.
416. Take the last four letters of 406 down and turn them into the past.
417. Never wrote vers libre.
418. Singularise, without authority, symbols of a jolly evening.
418a. The typist's curse.
419. The largest inhabitants of a South American Republic.

In 1940, Sir Max Beerbohm wrote to *The Times* with the following dreadful suggestion:

'No doubt you, like most people, have sometimes thought of some utterly awful thing that you *could* do if you chose to, some disastrous and devastating thing the very thought of which has brought cold sweat to your brow? And you may have at some time thought: "Suppose I released into the columns of *The Times*, one of these fine days, a crossword puzzle with clues signifying nothing whatsoever," and may have hideously pictured to yourself the effect on all educated parts of Great Britain? You may incidentally have seen yourself going into your club shortly before luncheon time and observing in the armchairs men with blank, set, fixed, pale, just-not-despairing faces, poring over the current issue? – one of them perhaps rising unsteadily and lumbering out of the library and asking the librarian, "Have we a Wordsworth concordance?" – or some question of that sort. You may have figured this man going home at tea-time, and his wife saying, "Oh, Stephen, is anything the matter?" He: "No, dear, nothing." She: "But you look so pale. You ———— ". He: "I've had a rather hard day, dear. But I'm quite all right."

'And you may further have wondered just how the apology in next day's issue should be worded – just what excuse should be offered, before the shutters in Printing House Square were briskly and slammingly put up for ever? Perhaps I oughtn't to remind you of this nightmare of yours. Forgive me.

'P.S. – The nightmare wouldn't be loathsomely complete unless a few of the clues were quite genuine – *and very simple*, so as to put the solvers in good heart, and make them confident of success, and keep their shoulders to the wheel. I have provided six such clues, with my usual forethought.'

The Times did run Beerbohm's impossible crossword. However, they must have felt that their readers had enough to worry about with a world war to occupy them, for they gave the game away by printing Sir Max's letter alongside.

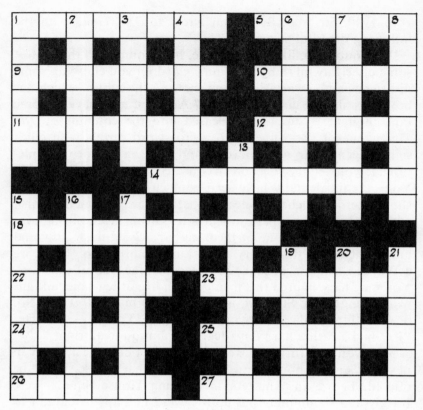

PUZZLE No. 52

Sir Max Beerbohm's Impossible Crossword for The Times

1. A Victorian states-
man lurking in a
side lair (8).
5. Milky way unseen
by star-gazers (6).
9. An insect with a
girl on each side
(8).
10. Pugilists' wear (6).
11. Four toes are
broken (8).
12. The cockney's god-
dess appears to
have been a
slimmer (6).

14. There's a little
company in the
meadow next
month (10).
18. 'But what if
memory Itself our
— —s had be-
trayed?' (Matthew
Arnold) (two
words (5, 5).
22. A nudist's aunt?
(6).
23. 'That day he ——
the Nervii'
(Shakespeare) (8).

24. Acknowledgement
of debt in a vessel
(6).
25. Neither animal
nor mineral, and
only three-fourths
vegetable (8).
26. Not what the
wicket-keeper tries
for in Essex (6).
27. The P.R.A. is
utterly confounded
(8).

1. Drum (Newbolt)
(6).
2. The top of the
morning, perhaps
(6).
3. A Manx beverage
(6).
4. Ho! Let's go in
(anag.) (10).
6. Wordsworth's fan
mail? (8).
7. And yet sugar *can*
be refined (8).
8. They are up and

doing, no doubt,
in 'the sweet o'
the year' (8).
13. Little Tommy
thought it meant
a red-faced black-
smith (10).
15. Voltaire's *prêtre
enragé* (8).
16. Such buns are
eaten on a good
day (two words)
(3, 5).
17. Caliban's sea-

change (8).
19. Pollarded haven
(6).
20. I'm in the old
Roman bath (6).
21. 'Our —— clues
that do but darken
counsel"
(Tennyson) (6).

13. Some Records

Large crosswords
In his spare time between 1938 and 1949, Robert Stilgenbauer of Los Angeles constructed a crossword with 3,185 down clues and 3,149 across. Although 125,000 copies were distributed, none has been returned completely worked out or even partially worked out.

(from Guinness Book of Records)

On Christmas Day, 1960, *The Observer* published a crossword containing 2,304 squares. On December 11th, 1969, *The Johannesburg Star*, *The Cape Argus* and *The Durban Daily News* gave readers until the end of the year to solve a crossword containing 793 across clues and 835 down clues – a grid requiring 7,347 squares. Prize for the first correct solution opened was approximately £100.

Fastest solver
Fastest solution to *The Times* crossword under test conditions was performed by Roy Dean, 43, of Bromley, Kent, in a BBC studio – on December 19th, 1970. His time: 3 minutes 45.0 seconds.

(from Guinness Book of Records)

Slowest solver
The Times received a communication in May 1966 from a lady in Fiji who had just completed the crossword set on April 4th, 1932.

(from Guinness Book of Records)

Shortest chapter in publishing history
This one.

Bibliography

There are scores of crossword puzzle collections and a goodly number of crossword dictionaries and similar aids to solving. Only the more significant ones are listed here.

The Crossword Puzzle Book. Plaza Publishing Company (Simon & Schuster), New York, 1924.
> The book that started the craze. Simon & Schuster published their 100th Crossword Puzzle Book in 1970.

The World's Best Word Puzzles. H. E. Dudeney. 124pp. 'Daily News', 1924.

The Quickway Key for Cross Words Solutions. H. W. Hill. 138pp. Warne, 1925.
> The first of many crossword guides.

The Torquemada Puzzle Book. E. Powys Mathers. 320pp. Gollancz, 1934.
> This contains the remarkable detective story 'Cain's Jawbone' designed in wrong page order. Why not write to Gollancz and request them to reprint it?

Crossword Golf. J. N. Rebar. 95pp. Rich & Cowan, 1933.
> Described as a game for two players.

Crossword Mystery. E. R. Punshon. 288pp. Gollancz, 1934.
> An ingenious murder story in which a crossword provides the clues to the crime.

'Cross-Sums' – A New Pastime. D. Whitelaw. 63pp. Bles, 1935.

The Strand Problems Book. W. T. Williams & G. H. Savage. 158pp. Strand Magazine, 1935.

The U.P.L. Cross-Figure Puzzle Book. S. C. Johnson. 59pp. Universal Publications, 1937.

112 Best Crossword Puzzles. Torquemada (E. Powys Mathers). 378pp. Pushkin Press, 1942.

The Penguin Problems Book. W. T. Williams & Savage. 156pp.

Penguin Press, 1940.

Verba Quadrata. G. S. Conway. 56pp. Blackie, 1942.
Crosswords in Latin.

How to Make Crosswords. T. A. Bott. 40pp. Quality Press, 1944.

The Second Penguin Problems Book. W. T. Williams & G. H. Savage. Penguin Press, 1944.

Findon's Crossword Companion. A. C. Findon. 67pp. Findon Publications, 1945.

Armchair Crosswords. Afrit (A. F. Ritchie). Warne, 1949.
To discourage cheating, a gummed seal had to be broken before you could see the solutions. The British Museum's copy remained intact until as late as 1973 when one of the library staff opened the seal.

Crosswords For You. F. G. Dulley. 64pp. Lucifer Press, 1947.

Word Play. Hubert Philips. 128pp. Penguin Books, 1945.

X-Word Pointer. All-Square. 80pp. County & Sporting Publications, 1949.
Subtitled: 'How to Win Prize-Money Crosswords'.

Story of the Jaxsquare. John Matthews. 104pp. John Wilson, Crosby, 1960.

Oddities & Curiosities of Words of Literature. C. C. Bombaugh. 375pp. Dover Publications, New York, 1961.
A modern edition of 'Gleanings for the Curious from the Harvest-Fields of Literature' published in 1890, with extensive annotations by Martin Gardner. Nothing on crosswords, but an invaluable source book of literary curiosities.

Anatomy of the Crossword. D. St. P. Barnard. 158pp. Bell, 1963.
Essential reading for anyone thinking of compiling crosswords, as is the next book.

Ximenes on the Art of the Crossword. D. S. Macnutt. 175pp. Methuen, 1966.

Solutions

Puzzle 1

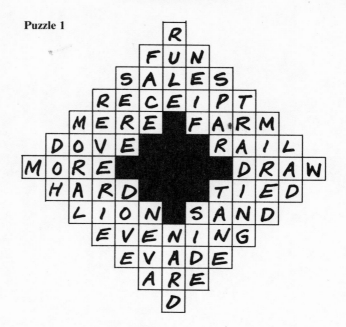

Puzzle 2

Puzzle 3

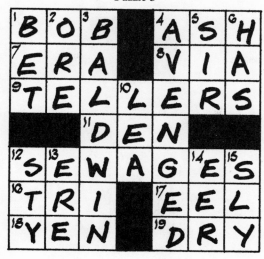

Puzzle 4   THE WORDS

London's the 'world in little'; 'make a
note on't,' Thames is its – cesspool;
that's the long and short on't."

THE LETTERS

At State receptions in day's untaxed
  Light,
Are *Ostrich* plumes a fair and goodly
  sight.
The *Neva* with old Thames will ne-ver
  cope,
Though *Despotism* dwell in Naples soap.
As for poor Cook? *O-why-hee* must
  excuse
The tale of his sad fate; 'tis now no
  News.

```
L   i   g   h   T
O   s   t   r   i c H
N     e   v   a   A
D e s p o t i s M
O – w h y – h e E
N   e   w   S
```

161

Puzzle 5

```
N   a p l e        S
.E    l b          E
W   a s h i n g t o   N
C   i n c i n n a t   I
A   m s t e r d a     M
S   t a m b o u       L
T     o r n e         A
L     e p a n t       O
E     c l i p t i     C
```

Puzzle 6   1,024 ways.

Puzzle 7

```
P A L A T E D
A N E M O N E
L E V A N T S
A M A S S E S
T O N S U R E
E N T E R E R
D E S S E R T
```

The verb 'palate': to perceive by the taste, to relish, has the authority of Shakespeare. 'Not palating the taste of her dishonour' ('Troilus and Cressida,' Act IV, sc. i; also 'Antony and Cleopatra,' Act V, sc. 2, seventh line). To 'levant' is, of course, to abscond dishonourably.

Puzzle 8   There are 372 ways of spelling 'Red Rum', all ending at the centre of the diamond. Clearly, there are just as many ways of spelling 'Murder'. Therefore, the square of 372 gives the total number of ways of spelling the complete phrase. 138,384 ways.

Puzzle 9   Many good mathematicians fall into the error of attempting to solve this on the basis of there being 24 starting points and the same number of endings. They reason that the square of 24, that is 576 different ways, will be the correct answer. They overlook the branch routes which give exactly 252 ways of reaching the centre, C, and as there are as many ways of getting back to the W's, the square of 252 gives the correct answer. 63,504 different ways!

162

Puzzle 10

```
        M
      C I T
    P A L E T
  H O R I C O N
    D E T U R
      T I M
        A
```

Puzzle 11

Puzzle 12

Puzzle 13

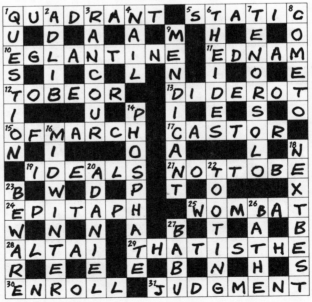

Puzzle 14

Puzzle 15

¹C	²A	³R	⁴B	⁵O	⁶N	⁷T	⁸I	⁹M	¹⁰R
¹¹O	C	E	A	N	S	¹²H	¹³E	E	D
									O
¹⁴R	E	V	¹⁵T	¹⁶I	¹⁷M	E	S	¹⁸C	I
									T
¹⁹D	U	E	T	²⁰N	O	R	A	H	²¹T
									A
²²A	²³P	R	E	S	U	M	E	²⁴A	E
									T
²⁵X	I	S	²⁶R	E	S	O	²⁷U	N	D
									E
²⁸E	N	E	I	²⁹T	E	S	T	I	N
									³⁰G
³¹S	K	³²I	E	D	³³S	T	O	C	³⁴K
									U
³⁵L	I	D	S	³⁶S	T	A	P	³⁷L	E
									S
³⁸I	N	³⁹O	⁴⁰T	⁴¹I	E	⁴²T	I	A	R
									T
⁴³O	G	L	E	S	⁴⁴P	⁴⁵S	A	M	B
									O

Puzzle 17

```
J E M I M A O B A D I A H
O L I V E R T A H E L B E
N O C A B N A R D N O I Z
M O R N L O I N I R A G E
I P R E E L S A M O S A K
A B I N A D A B S W I T I
R O B E R T E A C L A U D
H I N L A I S A A C T Y
P T O L E M Y I S N A K E
E U R I P I D E S D N A S
```

NOTES

Across: 15 rev. Nonsense Songs,
Preface, 'He weareth a runcible hat';
19. Rand; 23. Ham. I, 1, 166; 25. Lion;
26. Love's Labour Lost, IV, 1, 79; 5;
28. Peer; 44 and 48. Lay about it;
53. The two Keans.

Down: 7 rev. and 5. Mote; 10. Lion;
18. Br. round lea; 21. I'm in D.S.,
Dal segno; 27. Francis Thompson,
Mistress of Vision, XIII; 36. Tut(or);
41. D-yes; 43. Ancient Mariner, II;
45 rev. Chick-pea, peahen; 50 and 47.
i.e. pouched rat.

⁷C	²H	³A	⁴R	⁵O	⁶N	⁷S	⁸H	⁹A	¹⁰D	¹¹E
¹²L	U	C	U	L	O	¹³H	E	R	¹⁴I	N
¹⁵O	¹⁶N	E	¹⁷N	D	R	E	¹⁸B	O	R	T
¹⁹S	T	Y	G	²⁰I	A	N	²¹R	U	C	²²S
²³E	²⁴F	²⁵A	S	²⁶S	E	²⁷L	E	N	E	E
²⁸C	O	²⁹N	³⁰V	³¹E	Y	E	D	³²D	³³C	K
³⁴R	R	I	E	³⁵B	A	W	³⁶I	³⁷T	³⁸H	I
³⁹O	G	⁴⁰S	T	⁴¹A	M	⁴²A	S	H	U	R
⁴³S	E	E	⁴⁴I	N	G	⁴⁵B	⁴⁶O	A	T	H
⁴⁷S	T	A	N	D	⁴⁸C	E	R	⁴⁹T	E	S

CONCEALED POEM

Stand close around, ye Stygian set,
  With Dirce in one boat conveyed!
Or Charon, seeing, may forget
  That he is old and she a shade.
  — *Walter Savage Landor*

NOTES

Across: 13. She, he-r, s-he; 21. *rev.*
Curs; 42. Anag., 1 Chron., ii, 24;
48 and 49. Anag., C trees.

Down: 2. Leigh Hunt; 6. No-Ra, Doll's
House; 18. Debr(ett); 25. xxiii, 23;
27. Lew Wallace; 28. Cross as two
sticks; 33. C-hut-e; 42. Abraham,
meaning.

Puzzle 19

The quatrain:
> May he be fattest of the fatted kine,
> This newborn calf, this nineteen-
> thirty-nine,
> And make us quite forget the lean
> and late
> And unlamented nineteen-thirty-
> eight.

Across: 12 rev. Va-Grant; 16. Wife,
rhyming slang, 'trouble and strife,' and
then simply 'trouble'; 17. Shropshire
Lad, XXVII; 19. Luke XVI, 3; 25 rev.
T-ice; 27 rev. Luke XI, 42, famous
concocters of mint juleps; 29 rev and
14. Wolfe T.; 33 rev. Suttee; 42 rev.
D-aunt.

Down: 2 rev. A.A., cab; 3. Fr.; 11 rev.
Pongee; 23. Heraclitus; 26 rev. Tett
(IX); 31 and 32. Sitter; 35. See Brown-
ing, Garden Fancies, II, 55; 37 rev.
Mail; 40 rev. Hen-hussy; 42 rev.
Shropshire Lad, L.

Puzzle 20

¹N	²I	³O	⁴H	⁵T	⁶I	⁷N	⁸G	⁹A	¹⁰L	¹¹E	¹²J	¹³I	¹⁴G
¹⁵O	N	¹⁶H	C	U	S	N	O	N	¹⁷A	M	A	L	L
¹⁸S	A	¹⁹M	²⁰S	P	²¹E	E	D	A	²²S	O	²³U	S	A
²⁴A	²⁵E	A	P	P	O	P	²⁶I	F	S	²⁷L	R	I	D
²⁸G	I	²⁹G	U	E	³⁰N	³¹B	³²V	O	Y	A	G	³³E	S
³⁴R	P	³⁵A	R	R	³⁶Y	³⁷O	A	T	³⁸S	³⁹S	E	I	T
⁴⁰A	⁴¹T	U	⁴²G	A	M	⁴³J	⁴⁴E	⁴⁵S	A	P	⁴⁶P	H	O
⁴⁷D	A	N	⁴⁸T	⁴⁹E	M	⁵⁰S	E	U	L	⁵¹B	⁵²O	⁵³N	N
⁵⁴E	N	T	⁵⁵R	H	I	⁵⁶A	L	M	⁵⁷S	⁵⁸A	L	E	E
⁵⁹E	G	⁶⁰B	A	C	H	R	⁶¹J	O	A	N	⁶²K	R	⁶³I
⁶⁴D	O	R	C	A	S	⁶⁵A	E	C	I	D	A	O	B

NOTES

Across: 17 *rev.* Belloc, More Beasts,
The Llama; 18. Mas; 20. A Song of
Speed, 8; 26. Fr., 'ifs and ans';
32. Tours; 35. Arr(a)y; 37. Wild,
'feel their oats'; 42 *rev.* Gam; 62 *rev.*
D-irk and R. K.

Down: 4 *rev.* Bull in a china shop;
10. Kingsley, The Old Song, 3; 12 and
13. Ja-ils, Ger., Fr.; 23. Grue; 25 *rev.*
The coin; 29. G-aunt; 44 *rev.* Richard
and Francis; 45 *rev.* In Milton's C.;
48 *rev.* In the cart, in the soup; 49 *rev.*
Ache(ron); 60 and 54. Kim, xii.

Puzzle 21

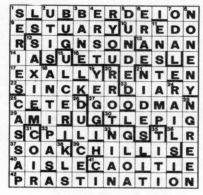

S	L	U	B	B	E	R	D	E	I	O	N
E	S	T	U	A	R	Y	U	R	E	D	O
R	S	I	G	N	S	O	N	A	N	A	N
I	A	S	U	E	T	U	D	E	S	L	E
E	X	A	L	L	Y	R	E	N	T	E	N
S	I	N	C	K	E	R	D	I	A	R	Y
C	E	T	E	D	G	O	O	D	M	A	N
A	M	I	R	U	G	T	L	E	P	I	G
S	C	P	I	L	I	N	G	S	T	L	R
S	O	A	K	C	H	I	L	L	I	S	E
A	I	S	L	E	C	A	O	I	T	I	E
P	R	A	S	T	I	N	A	T	I	O	N

NOTES

Across: 1. *gull*; 9. anag. and lit.;
13. an=if; 14. *guan*; 16. (consu)etudes;
17. *tern*; 21. *ka*, s.v. kae; 22. *glede*;
25. *rotch*; 29. Hudson, Rima; 30. *ruff*;
32. *lory*; 36. *emu*; 40. (P)aisle(y);
41. *pern*; 42. *roc*: 't. of time'.

Down: 1. *mina*: semies, rani; 3. *knot*;
5. *rhea*; 6. era(sed); 8. *tit*; 11. ens-
tamp; 12. *colin*; 15. anag. and lit.;
18. Herod, Salome; 20. *pie*;
21. n-l'd-es(t); 24. 3 mngs.; 25. *ree*: saree
=sari; 26. dull-sit; 28. *crow*; 31. co-i-r;
33. *dodo*: Ian C.; 34. *rype*; 38. *erne*.

Puzzle 22

171

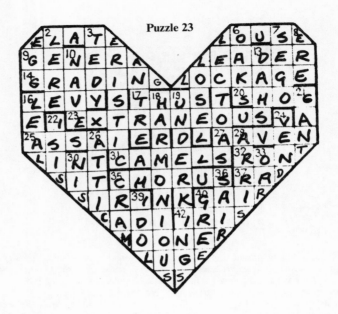

Puzzle 23

NOTES
Full answers to clues

Across: 1. Related; 5. Blouses;
9. Degenerate; 12. Leaseholder;
14. Degradingly; 15. Blockages;
16. Leavy; 17. Thalamus; 20. Shot-clog;
23. Extraforaneous; 25. Wassail;
27. Intravenous; 29. Splinter;
31. Cambrels; 32. Romaunt; 34. Visitor;
35. Chondrus; 37. Mirador;
38. Desiring; 40. Gambir;
41. Peccadillo; 42. Iritis;
43. Moonshiner; 44. Luggage.

Down: 1. Yeggs; 2. Lee-shore;
3. Tetrapody; 4. Manneristically;
5. Collectorship; 6. Oarlocks;
7. Serpigo; 8. Therein; 10. Native;
11. Cantref; 12. Filoselle;
13. Dahabiyahs; 16. Lethal;
18. Unharmoniously; 19. Undertakings;
21. Gallivant; 22. Isatis;
24. Lavender; 26. Brattices;
28. Engarrisons; 30. Tarnished;
33. Soare; 35. Cream; 36. Santir;
39. Eidola; 40. Grandee.

172

¹A	²C	³O	⁴U	⁵S	⁶T	I	C	⁷O	G	⁸L	⁹E
¹⁰U	I	S	T	¹¹O	¹²V	E	¹³R	¹⁴S	P	A	E
R	¹⁵T	A	G	R	A	G	¹⁶O	U	P	H	¹⁷E
¹⁸A	E	G	A	T	E	¹⁹S	²⁰S	E	C	²¹P	E
L	²²S	E	²³R	²⁴E	T	²⁵D	E	²⁶E	²⁷T	R
²⁸W	²⁹H	O	D	³⁰E	R	A	V	³¹D	I	S	C
³²E	O	³³A	³⁴N	³⁵A	N	Y	³⁶N	A	N	³⁷E	J
P	³⁸P	O	E	E	³⁹E	⁴⁰O	G	⁴¹O	S	W	⁴³I
⁴⁴S	O	H	W	⁴⁵H	⁴⁶G	⁴⁷O	⁴⁸T	⁴⁹C	T	⁵⁰E	N
⁵¹T	S	⁵²D	T	⁵³A	⁵⁴N	O	T	⁵⁵H	E	R	⁵⁶S
⁵⁷E	I	Y	⁵⁸S	D	⁵⁹G	N	E	⁶⁰O	⁶¹I	⁶²L	S
⁶³T	T	A	N	S	⁶⁴E	T	T	E	A	D	I

NOTES

Read forward and backward across the
diagonals until the shaded portion is
reached is the following limerick:

A curious tale at St. Ogg's
We hear – vice, a troop's padre, grogs.
   O see, Noote's heart's up leaped
   A new ditty they've cheeped –
No gas and no gaiters, no togs.

1. Acc. to us I.; 7. Shakespeare's
oeillade; 10. U is T, L is K, D is C;
14. S-p-ae; 15. Gar gat; 16. Goblin;
18. 241 B.C.; 20. S-Argo-ec, but 'sweet'
white wine in Masefield; 21. P.E.C. ten;
21. R-9. P in EEE; 22. S-err-E;
25. Tee-d; 30. V are; 31. Disc-harrow-
ing; 32. Hidden Act III, sc. 5; 36. No,
No, Nanette; 38. E. A. Poe; 42. S. W.
Inge; 59. Song – cf. Ours is a nice
house; 63. Natter; 39–65. Modern
Aegates, Adige.

1. A Ural; 2. CitEs; 3. (D)osage;
4. So(sma)rtie; 12. Anag. Ave;
19. Longfellow's Excelsior; 28. Result
of 'reach' (retch); 29–62. HO(L)D;
41. Octett; 41–23. (T)ocrea(T)e.
47. Kipling 'Oonts' (camels);
52. D(r)yads.

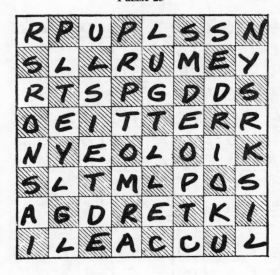

Puzzle 26

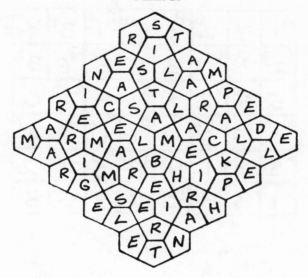

NOTES

Horizontal hexagons: 1. Stir; 2. Sane;
3. Lama; 4. Rice; 5. Last; 6. Pear;
7. Rama (St. Matthew II, 18);
8. Lame; 9. Mace; 10. Dell; 11. Grim;
12. Herb; 13. Pike; 14. Lese; 15. Hair;
16. Tern.

Vertical hexagons: 1. Emir; 2. Case;
3. Mars; 4. Silt; 5. Lamb; 6. Eire;
7. Alar; 8. Heir (*Heir of Redclyffe* –
C. M. Yonge); 9. Calk.

Boundary Words: 1. Stampede;
2. Elephant; 3. Telegram; 4. Mariners.

175

Puzzle 27

A 1	7	2 b	B c 6	9 d	C 1 e	3 f	4
D 2 g	1	E 7	3	F 8	5	G 5	9 h
H 5	6 k	J 2	8	K 1	8	L m 3	0
M 4 n	0	N 3 p	7	P 1	1 q	Q 3	4 r
R 8	2 t	S 1	9 v	T w 9	3	U x 1	2
V 1	3	5	W 2	7	X 3	5	3

NOTES

Equations (12) and (13). E and w are primes of the form $24n + 1$.

Equations (1) – (9). The formulæ used for the equation

$$a^3 = b^3 + c^3 + d^3$$ were

$$a = 6x^2 - 4xy + 4y^2$$
$$b = 3x^2 + 5xy - 5y^2$$
$$c = 4x^2 - 4xy + 6y^2$$
$$d = 5x^2 - 5xy - 3y^2$$

176

Puzzle 28

3	2	1	0	7	5	3	2	8	6	9	4
2	5	8	8	0	4	1	6	3	2	4	8
1	0	3	5	8	3	5	4	6	9	1	6
0	5	7	4	9	0	1	7	5	2	1	5
4	6	1	5	0	9	1	5	7	3	0	2
8	7	2	3	3	5	9	1	7	5	0	5
5	2	8	5	9	3	1	3	3	8	1	7
7	4	9	0	7	1	1	4	8	1	3	8
6	8	0	5	7	3	8	1	2	8	9	4
1	4	7	2	6	1	4	9	6	2	3	1
9	2	9	2	1	9	0	2	7	8	1	9
8	4	7	5	8	7	0	9	7	4	6	6

177

A^M	N^O	E^P	P^Q	H^R	A^S	N^T	T^U	I^V	Q^W	U	E^X
E	L	E	P	H	A	N	T	I	Q	U	E
BC	E	L	L	A	R	I	A	T	U	R	N
CH	A	M	A	N	A	C	R	E	I	G	N
DI	R	O	N	S	N	E	E	R	N	E	E
EN	U	R	S	E	S	U	M	A	T	R	A
FI	N	O	T	T	E	R	S	T	A	N	G
GD	I	S	E	A	R	O	E	E	L	E	O
HA	C	E	R	B	I	P	E	D	A	M	N
IN	A	N	N	A	N	E	R	E	C	U	E
JC	U	R	A	T	E	D	A	B	U	T	S
KE	S	O	T	E	R	I	C	A	N	E	T
LR	E	L	E	G	A	T	E	R	A	S	S

NOTES

B1. seller; 2. lasso. and anag.;
3. 4 meanings; C1. Esther, VII, 9;
3. Niger; D1. Irons (Ides); 2. Sneerwell
(Sheridan); 3. =eagle; E2. sum atra;
G1. Dis aliter visum; 2. Ares anag.;
5. Leo (nine); H1. Ace-R.B.; brace
anag.; 2. of two feet; 3. dam(n);
J1. two meanings; Q=cu-rate; 4. but
in as; L2. are reversed; 3. Mol(ass)es;
M1. Sea-urchin; and anag.; 2. J.
Campbell; N1. How pleasant etc.;
2. 'Time, time, time', The Bells, Poe;
3. 'It is the cause'; O2. Mor(o)se=sea-
horse; P2. row backwards; 3. turn
eight; Q1. league; 3. Greek letter;
4. teg(men); R. rana anag.; 2. answer
in; S2. Cycle (cyclic arrangement) of
Cathay; T1. Rate anag.; 3. Overseer or
rees; 4. Root of an acre.

Puzzle 30

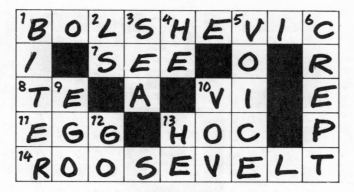

This solution was offered by the
Ministry of Home Security (Intelligence
Branch) Report H.S.I. 119/2 of
November, 1944.

Puzzle 31

179

Puzzle 32

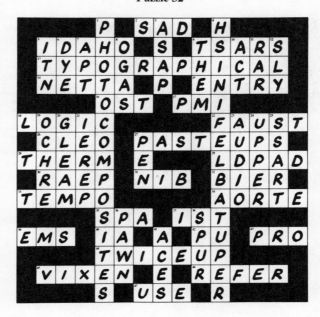

Puzzle 33

Alfred Lord Tennyson 'Ulysses'

And tho'
We are not now that strength which in old days
Moved earth and heaven; that which we are, we are;
One equal temper of heroic hearts,
Made weak by time and fate, but strong in will
To strive, to seek, to find and not to yield.

Puzzle 34

Nell Dunn 'The Incurable'

She had always cared about thinking,
hung onto thought as an important
thing in her life, but suddenly she
found it no longer mattered to her –
she simply ceased to bother.

Puzzle 35

```
H I P P I C
O     D     O
R E A S O N
A     D   I T
T A P I R
I               A go
S U             C h
    S U M M I T
```

Notes: (Uprights) Horatius: *Lays of Ancient Rome.*
Contract (Bridge).
(Lights) 3. Anagram of SO NEAR.
4. Add it!
5. Anagram of I PART.

Puzzle 36

```
A   L I P E D
T U S I T A L A
T   A K I N
E P I S T O L I C
N   O     S     E
```

Notes: At-ten-dance.
(1) Wing-footed.
(2) Name by which Stevenson was known to
the natives of Samoa.
(4) Contains 'pistol.'
(5) Lear's Nonsense Song.

Puzzle 37

```
S   T R I   P
C R A N E
R A N G E
A   C T O   R
P   E S T   S
```

Puzzle 38

```
T O R C H        C L I M B
A Z U R E        R E N A L
L O P E R        U V U L A
K N E A D        M E R E S
S E E M S        B L E S T
```

181

Puzzle 39

Puzzle 40

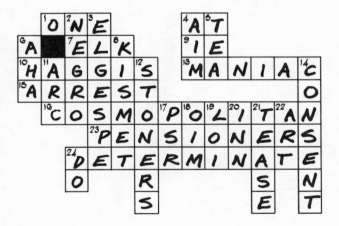

182

Puzzle 41

Note that each word appears twice,
under different definitions.

Puzzle 42

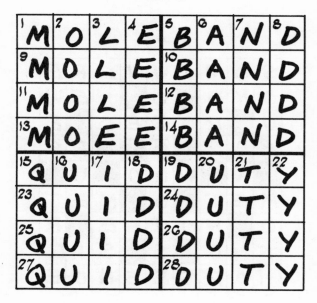

Puzzle 43

From 10 *across*, 1 *ac.* is a square
number, and is therefore 1849, 10 *ac.*
being 43. Therefore (as Mr. Turtle was
born in November) 9 *ac.* is 84, 3 *down*
is 48, and 7 *d.* is 64.

1 *d.*, beginning with 1 and ending
with 8, must be 1728, the only cube
number fulfilling the conditions.

As 4 *ac.* beings with 7 and ends with
8, its middle figure must be 3 to give a
multiple of 9.

As 6 *ac.* is a multiple of 11 and the first
two figures are established as 26, its
last figure must be 4.

5 *d.*, Baby Bert's age (born when Mr.
Turtle was 82 – see 4 *ac.*) is a number of
days ending in 3, and is less than 730
days by a number exceeding 36 and
less than 43 (see dates of Mr. Turtle's
death and Bert's birth). This number
must be 37, giving Bert's age as 693
days.

Puzzle 44

184

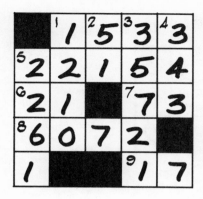

NOTES

4 *down* (cube of prime, and cannot end in 5, as 7 *across* is prime) is 343.

6 *across* must end in 1 (to make 1 *across* end in 3) and is a multiple of 7; so it is 21.

1 *down*, ending in 0 (multiple of 10) has for its first three figures **1, a square number, and is therefore 1,210 (3,610, or greater, would give a 3-figure value for 1 *across* ÷ 21).

3 *down* is $(21 \times 9)^2 = 35,721$. Hence 1 *across* is $21 \times 73 = 1,533$.

Eleven times any possible year of purchase must begin with 2. The subtraction of 1,210 from 5 *across* will not alter its first figure, which is therefore 2. And 5 *across* is a multiple of 11 (year × 11 + 1,210), which gives 1 as its middle figure.

9 *across* is therefore 17 (one-third of 51), and the year of purchase is 1904.

Time of ownership = 1915–1904 = 11 years.

5 *down* (22**) is a multiple of 17 and 19 (= 323), and can only be $323 \times 7 = 2,261$.

∴ 8 *across* (multiple of 11) has 7 for its third figure, giving $6,072 = 11 \times 23 \times 24$.

Hence I was 24 in the summer of 1904, and was therefore 61 in February, 1941.

Puzzle 46

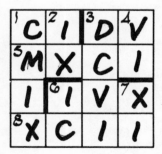

NOTES

Since there exist only two cubes of two digits, the puzzle must contain at least two cubes of more than two digits. Now 1 *down* cannot be cube as well as square (i.e., 729), for 1 *across*, being a factor of 3 *down*, cannot begin with 7. And 7 *across* cannot be a cube, for its digits add up to 15. Similarly, 9 *across*, which is 7 *across* divided by a two-figure prime, cannot be a cube. Therefore 2 *down* and 6 *down* are cubes.

Since 1 *across* is prime, 2 *down* can only be one of 125, 343, 729; if 4 *across* ended in 2, 5 *across* would end in 3, and 6 *down* be 343, which has no factor ending in 2; therefore 2 *down* is 343.

It follows at once that 6 *down* is 512, 4 *across* is 64, 5 *across* is 65, 1 *across* is 13 and 1 *down* is 169.

Now 7 *across* is 93*1, and must be 9321; whence 9 *across* is 717.

3 *down* (mult. of 13) must be 26; and as we have so far only two squares, 3 *across* must be 25.

Puzzle 47

NOTES

ACROSS

1. 101; H.C.F. of 505 and 606.
3. 505; difference of 606 and 101.
5. 1091; $101 \times 10 + 81$.
6. 16 (*rev.*).
8. 92; $101 - 9$.

DOWN

1. 909; 101×9.
2. 9.
6. 99; 9×11.
3. 606; 101×6.
4. 6; $\frac{1}{2}$ of $\sqrt{16 \times 9}$.
7. 11; $(505 + 606) \div 101$.

W	R	E	X	H	A	M		S	T	U	P	I	D	S
R	L		U	O		T		N		N		N		O
O	B	E		M	E	C	H	A	N	I	C	A	L	S
N		Y		A		H		N		O		C		T
G	R	E	E	N	L	A	N	D		N	O	T	C	H
		N		I		S		S		O		E		E
R	E	S	I	S	T	A	N	C	E		A	N	O	N
E			T		S		A		S					E
S	A	N	S		P	A	Y	P	A	C	K	E	T	S
T		E		E		M		R		L				
R	I	O	T	S		A	B	A	N	A	U	S	I	C
I		Z		S		L		M		P		M		A
C	O	O	P	E	R	A	T	I	V	E		E	T	U
T		I		N		D		S		I		R		S
S	O	C	I	E	T	Y		S	U	F	F	E	T	E

NOTES

10 Across. Shakespeare, Midsummer
Night's Dream.
20 Down. Mrs. Humphrey Ward.

NOTES

First puzzle:
23 Down. See Keats' Lamia.
24 Down. See Alice's Adventures in
Wonderland, Chapter 3.

Second puzzle:
21 Across. See Encyc. Brit.

Puzzle 50

S	R	E	D	H	E	R	R	I	N	G	
T	E	I	L	O	I	S	U	P			
R	N	S	P	I	F	L	I	C	A	T	E
E	G	M	A	S	D	S	E	B	A	L	A
L	E	A	T	H	E	R	J	A	C	K	E	T
I	L	H	Q	N	E	Q	R	H	Y		
T	H	I	E	F	I	V	I	G	A	R	M
Z	A	M	O	U	S	E	E	A	C	O	
R	B	H	R	Y	M	E	R	N		
A	D	D	R	E	S	S	A	M	E	N	T
T	O	T	B	E	H	B	B	H		
J	I	M	M	Y	O	G	O	B	L	I	N	S
A	A	M	C	O	M	A	T	E		

NOTES

The Listener regretted that none of its readers connected Lombardy and 'Man of Words' with *The Cardinal's Snuff-box* (23 Across), so that no completely correct solution was received for this competition puzzle. MEGA (in Abyssinia) was considered a fair attempt for 13 Across, or even TELA ('darts' for the game and 'spider's web' for Afrit's habitat).

Across: 8. Anag. *tile*; 11. Spite, Calif.; 12. Anag. *games*; 13. Anag. *base*; 14. Anag. *Taj-el-Rekah, etc.*; 18. 'Plum-stones' series; 23. Harland, Cardinal's Snuff-box; 24. Scandinavian mytholoty; 28. Anag. *Teman*; 29. Otbeh and Reyya.

Down: 3. Lohengrin; 4. Denis; 5. Browning, Hervé Riel; 6. Viscacha, cachalots; 7. Thackeray, Mr. and Mrs. Frank Berry; (10) Bab, Perils 'of Invisibility; 15. 'The Food of the Gods'; 21. Kamar-ez-Zeman and the Princess Budur; 25. Anag. *blame*; 30. Milne, When We Were Very Young.

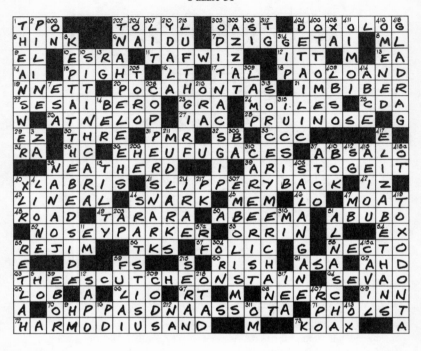